A PORTF
HEANOR AND DI
1900 – 2004

Heanor Market Place from tower of Parish Church, c1910.

Heanor and District Local History Society

www.heanorhistory.org.uk

CONTENTS

INTRODUCTION

The twentieth century saw more changes in the lives of people than any other one hundred years of our history. There were huge advances in medicine, education, science and technology, employment and the use of leisure time to name just some of them. Even in the small Derbyshire town of Heanor events of the time affected the day to day lives of the people, whatever their background. One hundred years ago the town was enjoying a period of prosperity as its many local industries provided employment for its inhabitants, new schools meant a brighter future for its children and the many churches and chapels played an important part in people's lives. Heanor Urban District Council had succeeded the former Local Board in 1895 and, as well as Heanor itself, covered the surrounding villages of Aldercar, Langley Mill, Langley, Marlpool, Loscoe and Codnor.

Heanor town centre had been recently developed following the sale of the grounds of Heanor Hall. This had allowed a new Market Place to be opened in 1894 and new streets laid out, with Market Street becoming an important new shopping area. Mundy Street, Godfrey Street and Ray Street comprised mainly residential properties, but also contained a few small business premises. Towards the end of the nineteenth century Heanor and the district around it had become an important manufacturing area with a wide variety of industries. I and R Morley had built a large textile factory in Heanor in 1875, extending it on many occasions, and by 1900 they were employing over one thousand people. There were many coal mines in the area, providing work for thousands of men and boys, while at Langley Mill were located Lovatt's Pottery, Smith's flour mills, Turner's engineering works and Pickersgill and Frost, manufacturers of fire grates.

Claud Corfield was the rector of Heanor (1886 – 1911) and worked tirelessly in the parish establishing mission churches and elementary schools. Heanor had once been a very extensive parish but in 1844 had been reduced in size with the formation of a new parish for the growing villages of Codnor and Loscoe, served by St James' Church at Crosshill. Other churches were to follow as each local community grew - Aldercar in 1871, and others early in the twentieth century at Marlpool, Langley Mill, Langley and finally Loscoe in 1938. Nonconformism was also strong in the area with each denomination having its own place of worship. The Methodists formed the largest group and each of its different Societies had their own place of worship, being particularly strong in Heanor, Langley Mill and Codnor. The Baptists, Congregationalists, Roman Catholics, Society of Friends and others also had their many followers throughout the area.

One hundred years ago communication links were primarily by train, canal, carriers' carts or private horse-drawn vehicle. The internal combustion engine was yet to establish itself. Heanor had two railway stations, one off Derby Road on the Great Northern Railway line to Ilkeston and the other off Midland Road on the Midland Railway line between Langley Mill and Ripley. Other local stations were at Langley Mill, Marlpool and Crosshill.

As the twentieth century progressed further developments in public services took place to improve people's lives. A piped water supply and electricity services were installed and a telephone exchange was opened in Langley Mill. In 1913 Heanor became an important point on the electric tram route between Ripley and Nottingham, with Langley Mill becoming the depot for the tramcars. The growing importance of the town was shown by a royal visit in June 1914 when crowds lined the streets to welcome King George V and Queen Mary. According to a local journalist, the scene was one which 'had never been equalled in the annals of Heanor'.

However, only a few months later Britain was at war with Germany resulting in many men from the district losing their lives fighting in Europe. As a fitting tribute to their sacrifice a memorial hospital was built, opening in 1926, and is still playing an important part today in the welfare of the local people. Heanor had its own local hero in Sergeant William Gregg, who, due to his actions in the War, became the first British soldier ever to receive the three highest awards for gallantry, the Military Medal, the Distinguished Conduct Medal and the Victoria Cross.

Improvements in the provision of a better education meant the building of new schools. A new secondary school building was opened in 1912 to replace the inadequate facilities provided in the former Heanor Hall, while three new schools for infants, boys and girls were built off Loscoe Road, opening in 1915. These new buildings were additional to the ones already in existence from the previous century, many of which were Church of England schools. In the second half of the twentieth century new secondary schools were built at Aldercar and Heanor Gate and older primary school premises were replaced by new buildings such as at Langley Mill and Coppice (Marlpool).

Life for many nearly one hundred years ago was hard with strict or harsh working conditions. An escape from the reality of daily life was provided by a visit to the cinema. The Empire Theatre opened in Red Lion Square, Heanor, in 1911, offering both stage shows and films. A cinema (later named the Ritz) opened at Langley Mill in 1916 and Heanor's second cinema, the Cosy, opened on the Market Place in 1922.

The death of Edward Miller Mundy in 1920 brought to an end the family's long association with the area. They were local benefactors and the largest landowners around Heanor. Their home was at Shipley Hall, set in a large estate on the southern outskirts of the town. Edward's son, Godfrey, on succeeding to the estate, decided not to live at Shipley Hall, thus ending an association with the area going back to 1729. Much of the family's wealth came from the coal mines on the estate, providing employment for thousands of men and boys. Control of the mines passed to the Shipley Colliery Company, set up to continue their development. Damage had been caused to Shipley Hall by mining subsidence and it was demolished in 1942, following unsuccessful attempts to sell it. Rubble from the building went to form part of the runway at an American airfield being built at New York, a village near Tattershall, Lincolnshire.

During the 1920s competition from the trams and the growing number of small bus operators led to the closure to passengers of Heanor's two railway stations, plus those at Crosshill and Marlpool, leaving only the one at Langley Mill open. The trams themselves ceased to run in 1932, being replaced the following year by trolley buses, which operated not only on the Ripley to Nottingham route, but also on a new route from Heanor to Ilkeston and Hallam Fields.

In the 1930s Heanor Urban District Council had outgrown its accommodation in the Town Hall. To solve the problem the Council in 1935 purchased Shanakiel, a large house on Ilkeston Road, continuing to use the Town Hall for some of its departments.

The Second World War led to the sending overseas of many men from the area, some never to return. Young men, known as Bevin Boys, were brought into the local mines from all over the country to maintain coal production.

Many local factories went over to war work, perhaps the most noteworthy locally being the new Vic Hallam premises at Langley Mill, which were occupied by Collaro Limited, manufacturing shells and munitions. The end of the War in 1945 was celebrated by many street parties and again the Council debated how to honour the fallen. It was decided to lay out a memorial park on land adjacent to Shanakiel. This was duly opened in 1951 by the 11th Duke of Devonshire. Also following the War, the Council was heavily involved in the provision of new homes, developing large council estates at Loscoe, Langley Mill and Marlpool.

Sadly the final years of the twentieth century were marked by a series of closures amongst the local industries, particularly the traditional one of coal-mining. By 1970 all the local mines had closed, the only coal produced since then being by the opencast method. Other local industries which closed were Morley's, Turner's, Hallam's, the Pottery and Aristoc. These firms had employed many thousands of local people, now it meant travelling further afield to seek work. The new companies set up on purpose-built industrial estates required a much smaller workforce than the older traditional industries.

From the 1960s onwards people were becoming more mobile and independent of public transport. Most families now owned a car and could travel to larger centres such as Derby or Nottingham for shopping and entertainment. This resulted in the closure of many shops in Heanor as well as its cinemas. Attempts were made to encourage people to shop locally, when larger food-stores were opened, firstly with Fine Fare (now Somerfield) on Market Street followed by the conversion of the Co-op store on the Market Place to food only. However, the latter closed in 2001, leaving the area with no Co-op premises for the first time in over one hundred and twenty five years. In 1999 Tesco opened a superstore on the Morley factory site and this was followed by other shops on the Theta Dyeworks site. Changes were also taking place in people's views on religion, falling attendances led to the closure of many chapels. St Lawrence's parish church, Heanor, was to undergo change too, for in 1981/82 its nave and chancel were demolished to be replaced by a more flexible contemporary structure, incorporating a church hall.

In 1974 Heanor Urban District Council amalgamated with the Councils of the three adjacent towns of Alfreton, Belper and Ripley to form Amber Valley District (now Borough) Council. Shanakiel became the Finance Department of the new authority until new headquarters were built in Ripley in 1993. Today some of the former Urban District areas have their own smaller local councils, such as Heanor and Loscoe Town Council, Aldercar and Langley Mill Parish Council and Codnor Parish Council. 1976 saw the opening of Shipley Country Park on the outskirts of Heanor and in 1986 several acres around Shipley Lake were developed, firstly as Britannia Park, and subsequently as the American Adventure theme park.

These are just some of the changes which have taken place since 1900, resulting in the town and district which we know today. Changes, of course, are still taking place, making it very difficult to say how the area will look in another one hundred years time. In the meantime the following chapters will attempt to show life over the past one hundred and four years, as it was recorded by many different photographers, to all of whom we owe our grateful thanks.

Brian Key
Tom Larimore
John Wright

CHAPTER ONE.
THE CHANGING SCENE.

In the Domesday Survey of 1086 Heanor is recorded as Hainoure, a name meaning 'high ridge' and it is an undeniable fact that the church and its surroundings occupy a dominant position overlooking the valley of the River Erewash. To the north and north-east the ground falls steeply away into the valley towards Loscoe and Langley Mill, but slopes away more gradually in other directions.

Historically, the area was predominantly agricultural, but to the north and south were two large estates, the former surrounding the medieval castle at Codnor and the latter around the eighteenth century Shipley Hall. The two main families at Codnor were the Greys and the Zouches, while Shipley was the home of the Miller Mundy family.

The growth of Heanor has differed from the more usual pattern of settlement, where a cluster of buildings surrounded the church and gradually spread outwards. Up to around three hundred years ago Heanor consisted of a number of isolated groups of cottages scattered amongst the fields, each little community having its own name, usually ending in 'town', such as Peacock Town or Bogard Town. Many of these had grown from an individual farm with neighbouring cottages for the workers. From the eighteenth century onwards, a rise in demand for coal led to the exploitation of the local rich seams and an influx of new labour. Terraces of red-brick houses for the workers were built, which in time linked together the former isolated settlements and created the present pattern of roads and streets.

Heanor's original business and shopping area was the upper part of High Street and from Red Lion Square to the higher parts of Derby Road, known locally as Tag Hill. The market was situated on a piece of ground alongside the Jolly Colliers public house. Following the development of the new Market Place site, and the establishment of Market Street as the main shopping outlet in the late nineteenth century, the business area moved away from Derby Road, although it still retained many small shops. In recent times there has been a further movement of the commercial centre to the High Street area following the opening of the Tesco store and other shops on the former Morley's site. The surrounding villages of Codnor, Loscoe, Langley Mill and Marlpool continue to retain their individual identities, although now linked to Heanor by ribbon development. Each village still has its own shopping facilities, although not as extensive as a hundred years ago when they were almost self-sufficient.

The original siting of the parish church on the ridge determined the location of the settlement of Heanor. Over the succeeding one thousand years the community has grown until now nearly all the available land has been filled with housing or business premises. Inevitably over the years some of the older buildings have been lost, causing sadness to older members of the community who mourn their passing. In this chapter we will take a photographic journey around the town of Heanor and its neighbouring villages to see how the built environment has changed between 1900 and the present day.

A tram waits on Heanor Market Place to leave for Nottingham on a quiet afternoon with few passengers about. An early motor car is parked behind the tram while a horse and cart stand by the memorial horse trough and drinking fountain. These were erected in 1887 to commemorate Queen Victoria's Golden Jubilee. The shops behind the tram were built in 1902 and named Burton Terrace, after George Burton, who lived at Laburnum House, the three storied white building.

6

Since its opening in 1894 the Market Place has been an important venue for assemblies of all kinds, both joyous and sombre. At the time of the First World War a large crowd has gathered to watch soldiers of the King's Royal Rifles, possibly on a recruitment drive. The large number of children present would suggest that they had come from a local school for the occasion.

A 1935 view across the Market Place on market day with a few shoppers browsing at the old wooden stalls. All the buildings remain today with little change, except for the former Co-operative premises to the right of the parish church. The Co-operative later took over the shops alongside. Some years afterwards the upper floor was removed and a flat roof fitted. Following closure of the Co-operative store in 2001 the building was acquired by the South East Derbyshire College and it is now the Heanor Learning Centre.

Moving from the Market Place to Market Street, and looking back towards the church, many people are out shopping. There is an absence of traffic in this 1920 scene, with not even a tramcar in sight, the only vehicles being a delivery van waiting by the kerb and a horse drawn cart approaching from the rear. Today all the properties on the left have been replaced by modern retail developments.

In a slightly earlier view than the previous one, possibly around 1910, we see the view down Market Street, then recently developed as the main shopping area. On the right is Crompton and Evan's Bank (now NatWest) opened in 1892 and just below it the alley leading to the offices of the Heanor Observer newspaper. One current retail absentee at that time was Woolworth's, who later opened in the building on the right with the high gable, then the Liberal Club.

The lower end of Market Street leads to Red Lion Square, named after the adjacent hotel. In this view of around 1910 the shops of Market Street continue to the right while on the left is a row of properties which would soon be demolished to make way for the Empire Theatre. The absence of traffic is again noticeable with pedestrians freely strolling around enjoying the good weather.

Ten years later and the Empire Theatre has become well established in Red Lion Square. Live stage shows were performed as well as the showing of films, but it is the latter that are being well advertised in this view. On offer at this time were "Slave Girl" and "Martin Numa – Detective", the latter claiming to be "Exclusive to this theatre". The theatre entrance then was in the short wall to the right of the advertisements and it was some years later that a grander entrance with a balcony was added to change considerably the appearance of the front façade.

The revised entrance to the Empire is clearly seen in this 1930 view of Red Lion Square. The pavements are busy with shoppers while an early omnibus awaits its next turn of duty. It belonged to Herbert Hall who provided a workers' service to the Celanese factory at Spondon. Until 1999 this was a busy junction, now the situation has eased with the building of a roundabout lower down High Street, making the road behind the photographer into a cul-de-sac.

Facing the other way from the previous photograph, Derby Road rises to an area known locally as Tag Hill, so named from the practice of attaching an extra horse to a team to pull loads up the steep slopes towards the town centre. To the right of the picture is the Red Lion Hotel, with stables adjacent, and further along the square frontage of Morley's Derby Road factory. On the left, shops continue the line round from Market Street to the original main shopping area of Derby Road.

Looking towards Red Lion Square from Tag Hill, Derby Road is virtually traffic free with only two vehicles to be seen, making it reasonably safe for the young boy on the left to be out alone. Apart from the group at the junction with Nook End Road below the Cross Keys public house, few others are out to enjoy the sunny weather. One of the houses beyond the group of bystanders was the home of Norah Carpenter, who gave birth to the Heanor quads in 1944.

The Jolly Colliers public house stands prominently to the right, carrying an advertisement for Horner's Weekly. Derby Road descends towards Heanor's Great Northern railway station before rising again towards Smalley. On the left may be seen the high gable of the Baptist Chapel, built in 1847. This area was formerly known as West Hill, and is still called that today by some older members of the community.

We return to Red Lion Square and see the view down High Street around 1910. The large building on the right is known as Regent House and at that time was partially used by Boots, on the first of three sites which they have occupied in Heanor. Beyond are a number of houses which have now been converted into small shops. The gable end of the National School is towards the end of the buildings to the right while the left side is dominated by the tall facade of Morley's factory.

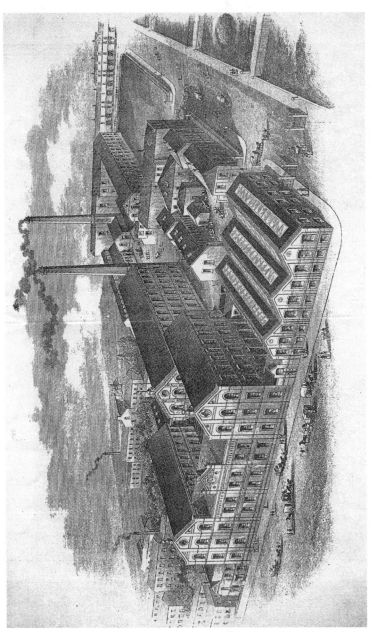

This line drawing shows the extent of Morley's textile factory around 1900. The main frontage is on to High Street, with the factory units extending behind it as far as Nelson Street. The first factory was begun in 1874, but there were many extensions to it, not only on this side of High Street but on the opposite side also with the building of a dyeworks and North Side, a long three storied factory block, housing more of the textile processes. In 1967 the firm became part of the Courtauld Group, but closed in the 1990s, then, following demolition, the site was developed for retail use.

Lower down the hill, the name changes from High Street to Loscoe Road, flanked by a mixture of domestic and business premises. Here a procession moves along Loscoe Road towards the town centre led by a brass band. A single deck trolley bus is held at the rear by the slow moving marchers. The Union flag draped from an upstairs window and the large crowd would indicate a day of importance, possibly the 1935 Silver Jubilee.

Moving towards Loscoe, the photographer has recorded a very rural looking Heanor Road in the early years of the twentieth century. A horse and cart makes its steady progress towards Heanor while a workman has time to stand and pose. The large property in the distance, known as Chaddesden House, was the home of Mr Gaunt, owner of Loscoe Brickworks, which were situated to the left of the white hut.

The centre of the village of Loscoe appears very quiet, allowing a few bystanders to pass the time of day undisturbed by any traffic. A pile of coal has been tipped at the roadside and waits to be taken in, it would not be a problem to passing vehicles when this picture was taken around 1910. The sheds to the right, on the forecourt of the Eclipse public house, were small shops, one of which was a butcher's. The building to the left was then a general store. Today, it is the village post office and shop, selling a wide range of items, such as groceries, newspapers, beer, wines and spirits.

A little distance from the main road through Loscoe is the dam, which has always been an attraction to local people, whether for fishing, bird-watching, picnicking, or even skating in the winter time. Some also used it for boating as seen in this 1924 photograph. It was not always such a tranquil spot for in 1582 it became the site of an ironworks, the waters being used to power the hammers and bellows. At its maximum it was twenty four acres in extent but today by infilling has been reduced to around eight acres.

The road from Loscoe leads via Crosshill to Codnor. This 1910 view shows some of the properties alongside Codnor Market Place before the line of buildings was complete, all later being for retail purposes. The large shop to the right, on the corner with Mill Lane, was Bostock's butchers, today it caters for the needs of anglers, after belonging for many years to Logic, retailers of electrical goods. The cottages in the far distance (Niffen's Row) have now been demolished and the adjacent busy junction is controlled by traffic lights.

Codnor Castle, about one mile from the village over fields, dates from around 1200, when it was occupied by one of the most powerful families in the land – the de Greys. They were succeeded by the Zouches but by the early 1600s the castle had been partially abandoned. The stone was sold off and used to build other properties in the neighbourhood. Only portions of the keep remain today, with some fragments of the inner wall.

The road from Codnor to Langley Mill through Woodlinkin follows a ridge of high ground so it is fully exposed to the worst kinds of weather. In the harshest of winters the road is frequently blocked by snow, blown into huge drifts by strong winds. When a bulldozer was brought in to clear these drifts in February 1979 a car was discovered, completely buried in the snow.

Aldercar Hall was built in 1668 by a member of the Burton family, but it passed through numerous other families before being bought by the Butterley Company of nearby Ripley. Francis Beresford Wright, Chairman of the Company from 1888 to 1911, lived at the Hall and was followed by his son, Arthur. On his death no further occupancy took place and it was demolished in 1962. A large new house has been built on the site.

Moving into Langley Mill we see the view along Cromford Road, one of its two main highways. It formed the first section of the 1766 Langley Mill to Cromford turnpike road, hence its name. Part of it became an important shopping area, particularly after the founding of the Langley Mill and Aldercar Co-operative Society in 1875. Its large retail, social and office premises, seen in the distance, came to dominate this part of Cromford Road. Following closure, parts of the building have been regenerated as the Bridge Centre, and they now have a valuable local community use.

Cromford Road is located in a low-lying part of Langley Mill, being not far from the course of the River Erewash. Until improvements were made to the river bed, flooding was a common occurrence. In 1932, a particularly bad year, the road and adjacent premises were flooded to a depth of several inches, as seen in this photograph. The two shops to the rear were Wyles' footwear and Phillips' cycles, with the Midland Hotel to the left (now renamed The Mill).

Cromford Road forms a junction with Langley Mill's other main road, Station Road. In this view taken at the junction around 1920 we see two of the village's important landmarks, the domed tower of the Wesleyan Chapel and the pottery kilns. No tramcars are in sight, just a horse and cart with one wheel running along the tram lines. Numerous small shops are in evidence, including the village post office next to the premises of Mr T.Cave, Draper and Outfitter.

The railway bridge over Station Road in Langley Mill, as seen in 1905, with a train waiting in the station. Between the road and the station approach may be seen the Boer War memorial on its original site. Leading off to the right, just before the bridge, is the way to the bay platform for trains to Heanor and Ripley, the path in use today for people catching trains to the north from the re-opened Langley Mill station.

A little further along Station Road, but still looking towards the railway, we see a line of shops on the left, some with their blinds down to protect goods on display from the sun. At the far end, behind the elegant tram standard, is the single-storey 1916 Ritz Cinema. It was later rebuilt with an inside balcony and re-opened in 1933, today it is the premises of Slater's Glass and Windows.

Closer to Heanor, but still on Station Road, around 1910 the whole has a peaceful air, with just a horse and cart in sight. This is in stark contrast to today's scene, when vehicles are parked in front of nearly all the houses and an almost constant stream of traffic rushes by. At least the cricket ground over the fence to the left still provides something of a green oasis.

Moving up the hill from Langley Mill to Marlpool we see the houses and businesses on Mill Road, all the buildings remain, but the shops have closed and been converted to houses. The sign over the building in the centre is for Wadkinson's the butchers, opposite to which was Collumbell's bakers. Nearby stood a windmill which ceased to grind corn in the 1870s. The contents of the mill were sold in 1885 and, following demolition of the shell in 1891, some of the bricks were used to build a nearby house.

Breach Road, Marlpool, facing the junction with Ilkeston Road. The sign hanging above the car is for the Queen's Head public house, while in the far distance is a farm house, demolished to make the present entrance into the Marlpool housing estate down Sunningdale Avenue. A number of small shops are in evidence as well as some of the locals, mostly children, who seem to be posing for the camera.

A 1920s view along Ilkeston Road showing it as a quiet tree-lined road linking Heanor to Marlpool and Ilkeston. Only three vehicles are seen on the road in marked contrast to today's heavy traffic. Behind the tall telegraph pole to the left may be seen the square tower of All Saints' Parish Church, Marlpool.

A tree-lined Ilkeston Road, formerly known as Sye Lane, makes a pleasant approach to Heanor from Marlpool. The three buildings in the centre of this view are the parish church, the Institute building and Ray Cottage. The Institute was an important meeting place for groups while Ray Cottage was once the home of John Milner, coachman to the Ray family of Heanor Hall.

Before returning to the Market Place, we note the view down Church Street, around 1910. The twin-gabled house in the centre was known as The Dene, home until his marriage of William Howitt, the Victorian writer. It was demolished in 1934, some of the other properties have also gone, but those on the left, nearest to the camera, remain.

Children and adults pose for the photographer next to the Old White Hart Inn, opposite Heanor parish church. Many aspects of the picture recall life of around one hundred years ago – the horse and dray, the push chair with its metal wheels, the style of dress and the gas lamp with its ornate iron bracket. All of the buildings on this side of the road were demolished in 1913 to widen the carriageway before laying down the tram lines.

CHAPTER TWO.
EDUCATION.

Over the past one hundred years many changes have taken place in the provision of education in Heanor and district. At the turn of the twentieth century the Church of England was providing most of the elementary education with a large number of schools throughout the area, such as Mundy Street and Commonside in Heanor, and others in Langley, Loscoe and Crosshill. There was also the National School on High Street, Heanor, as well as a number of small private schools.

For older pupils Heanor Technical School was opened in 1893 with Ralph Stoddard as its first headteacher. The school used the old Heanor Hall building and when that proved inadequate new premises were built, opening in 1912. As the century progressed the school name was changed, firstly to Heanor Secondary School, then Heanor Grammar School and currently to the Sixth Form Centre of the South East Derbyshire College The school offered an education leading to Further Education, such as University, Teacher Training College, etc.

The other schools too underwent periods of change as the range and methods in education broadened, plus coping with the gradual raising of the leaving age. In 1900 pupils left school at the age of twelve, in 1918 this was raised to fourteen, in 1947 to fifteen and in 1973 to its present level of sixteen.

To take one example of how local schools have changed, the schools off Loscoe Road, Heanor, have passed through many phases. There were originally three schools on the site, opening in 1915 – an infant school (which has remained unchanged), and separate boys' and girls' schools. By 1958 the latter two were catering for pupils between the ages of seven and thirteen, except for pupils who had transferred to Heanor Grammar School on passing their 11+ examination. Those remaining at Loscoe Road transferred at the age of thirteen to Aldercar Secondary Modern School for their final two years of education. Following reorganisation in 1958 the boys' school premises became the William Howitt Junior Mixed School while the girls' school premises became the Howitt Secondary Modern School. Six years later, all pupils at the age of eleven were transferred to a new secondary school which had opened at Heanor Gate, and were assessed there at the age of thirteen for a move to the Grammar School. The former Howitt Secondary classrooms then became part of the William Howitt Junior School.

Over the last thirty years some school premises have been demolished and their sites redeveloped. Amongst these are Aldercar Infant School, Langley Mill Boys' School, Crosshill Boys' School and Jessop Street School, Codnor. New schools, which have been built to provide more suitable accommodation, include the primary schools at Loscoe and Coppice (Marlpool) and the junior school at Langley Mill One loss in recent years has been the former mining college building on Ilkeston Road. This was built in 1930 and jointly funded by Heanor Urban District Council and the Miners' Welfare Fund. It was used latterly by the South East Derbyshire College but, following demolition in 2003/4, the site, and the adjacent playing fields, will be used for housing and a new Mundy Street Junior School. Despite these new projects, many local pupils will continue to be educated in quite old buildings, several of which have held celebrations to mark their centenaries.

As well as changes to the buildings there have been dramatic changes to the range of education provided and in teaching methods. Computers now play a large part in any student's education – a far cry from the days of blackboard and chalk. A further development has seen the renaming and change of emphasis of the two secondary schools – Aldercar is now the Aldercar Community Language College and Heanor Gate, the Heanor Gate Science College. Schooldays formed an important part of everyone's life, a time of memories, good and bad, and of friendships, some lasting all through life. Nearly everyone remembers the names of teachers who played a significant part in their time at school, perhaps guiding them towards a successful future career. And who can forget school dinners and swimming lessons at Langley Open Air Baths?

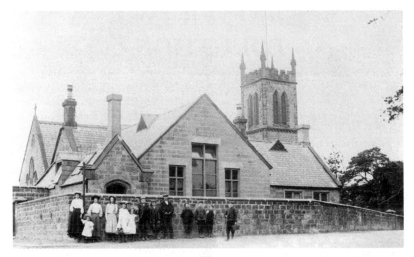

Crosshill School was erected in 1844 at the same time as the adjacent St James' Church. Initially it was for boys and girls from the Codnor/Loscoe area, but by 1875 it was for boys only. The girls went to a separate school on Jessop Street at Codnor. Crosshill eventually closed in 1964, followed by demolition early in the next decade, allowing an awkward road junction nearby to be improved. This view dates from around 1900.

The first headteacher at Crosshill was Mr Floyd Pine, who was followed by his son, Arthur. This photograph shows one of the classes in 1920. In the days before school uniform there was a wide range in the standard of clothing worn by the boys, reflecting the differences in the social classes in the Codnor area.

Commonside Infant School on Thorpes Road, Heanor, was one of the many schools built through the efforts of Canon Claud Corfield, vicar of Heanor, 1886-1911. It was opened in 1902, under its first headteacher, Miss E.Sykes, who admitted one hundred and seventy seven pupils on the opening day. In later years it was renamed Corfield Infant School and in 2002 its centenary was celebrated by the opening of a new classroom. This photograph is dated 1909.

In the years around 1900 many schools were built in and around Heanor, so that all children could receive a full-time education. Marlpool Boys' School opened in 1908 near to the junction of Breach Road and Claramount Road, and continues today as Marlpool Junior School. A notable headteacher was Mr Edward (Ted) Hollingsworth, who ran the school for thirty five years. A serious-looking class of boys are seen being photographed around 1910, soon after the school's opening.

This photograph is believed to have been taken in the school on Lacey Fields Road, Langley. It opened in 1871, but was enlarged in 1893 to take two hundred and seven girls and one hundred and twenty eight infants. Today the school is known as Langley Nursery and Infant School, accommodating pupils from pre-school age to seven years. Here a large class of girls are seen posing for the camera, many in the traditional pinafore dresses of a hundred years ago.

Lockton Avenue Junior Girls' School, Heanor, was a mainly wooden building with four classrooms, opened in 1928 on a site next to Beech Walk. Some of the staff over the years included Mrs Maud Meakin, Miss Dorothy Lomax and, probably its best known headteacher, Miss Ada Crumpton. The final headteacher before closure in 1962 was Mrs Hughes, who went on to become head at the newly built Coppice Primary School, Marlpool. The Lockton Avenue buildings were later demolished and homes built on the site.

Three schools off Loscoe Road, Heanor, for infants, boys and girls, opened in 1915, each with its own headteacher and staff. A Loscoe Road Girls School photograph of 1920 shows a class of thirty seven pupils, all looking rather serious. No class teacher is shown, which is rather unusual for a school photograph.

The staff at Loscoe Road Boys' School in the 1930s. The headteacher, Mr Charles Mettam, is seated front centre, with his daughter, Connie, front row left. (Charles Mettam died on the 23rd December 1950, aged 75 years). The other ladies, left to right, are Gladys Woolley, Ruby Robinson and Nellie Bancroft. The male staff are unknown, but the centre one may be Mr Hubert Chambers, who went on to become headteacher at the school until his retirement in 1962.

The Loscoe Road Boys' School choir around 1928 with their trophies. Left to right (standing) the boys are F.Stainsby, D.Sharpe, E.Allen, John Groves, W.Gillott, H.Tudor, J.Bestwick, Henry Smith, F.Gilman, E.Fowkes, ? Sellars, ? Cowlishaw, Clarence Draper, A.Smalley, W.Seal, J.Tudor, Charles Beresford, J.Cope, A.Bennett, A.Booth, E.Ratcliffe, and S.Pryor. Seated front row (left to right) are Harry Pollard, Eric Wilson, Miss G.Woolley (conductress), Mr C.Mettam (Headteacher), Miss C. Mettam (pianist), W.Buxton and F.Davies.

As well as a strong musical tradition, Loscoe Road Boys' School also did well in sport. The football team of 1947/8 is seen with Mr Maurice Brentnall (left), Mr Jasper Strover (headteacher) in the centre and Mr Foinette (right).
Back Row Standing: Derek Rowe, Keith Williams, Clarence Harvey, Jack Saxton and Keith Rowley.
Front Row Seated: Ronald Gillott, Roy Palmer, Ralph Evans, Colin Webster, Lawrence Harvey and Peter Richardson.

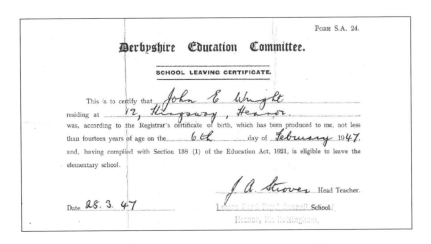

From September 1947 the school leaving age was raised from fourteen to fifteen years of age. John Wright's birthday was in February so, although still only fourteen, he was able to leave at Easter 1947, six months before the new higher leaving age was introduced. This is John's School Leaving Certificate signed by the headteacher, Mr J.A.Strover.

Most pupils will remember school visits, a break from the normal classroom routine. Originally visits would have been to local places of educational interest but soon moved on to extended journeys, including excursions abroad. In 1946 some of the boys from Loscoe Road School line up before setting off to Bakewell. The bus driver (left) is Mr Archie Fowkes and on the right is Mr Wood, a school governor.

The forty-eight boys of Mr Roy Thorpe's class 2A are seen at Loscoe Road Boys' School in 1955. Some of the names are, back row, left to right - Mr Hubert Chambers (Headteacher), Peter Woodward, Kenneth Meakin, David Winfield, Terrance Lloyd, Alan Turner, Michael Parkin, Michael Percy, David Woodcock, David Pugh, Melvin Clark, Mr Roy Thorpe (class teacher).

Next to back row ------ ,Peter Wilkinson, ------, George Osborne, Alwen James, Dennis Hartshorne, Peter Green, Nigel Abbott, Roy Thompson, Peter Brennan, Alistair Jefford, Geoffrey Patrick, John Poynton.

Next to front row - Alan Gillott, Robert Woolley, John Painter, David Bartlam, ------, Thomas Bridge, John Bailey, Alan Bamford, Peter Ludlam, Eric Draper.

Front row - Michael Fletcher, Peter Barry, Brian Brailsford, Colin Calladine, Peter Hadfield, Neville Sharpe, Roy Davis, Roy Cox, John Glenn, Malcolm Sharp, Kenneth Lilley, Ivan Moye, John Hill.

(Uncertain of names underlined).

In the summer of 1958 some of the pupils and staff from Loscoe Road Boys' School went on a ten day camping holiday to Cornwall and the south of England. The party is seen at Land's End, three hundred and thirty miles from Heanor. Staff from left to right on the back row are Mr R.Heathcote, Mr A.Priestley, Mr T.Close, Mr R.Morley, Mr M.Brentnall, Mr M.Green, Mr B.R.Key and Mr J.A.Ferraby.

In 1958 the separate Loscoe Road Boys' and Girls' Schools were reorganised into the William Howitt Junior Mixed School (seven to eleven years) and the Howitt Secondary School (eleven years onwards). The Secondary School staff are seen in 1963. Back row, left to right - Mr P.R.Crofts, Mr J.A.Ferraby, Mr T.J.Larimore, Mr M.Brentnall, Mr I.D.McIntyre, Mr K.Matthewman, Mr G.A.Swift. Front row - ------ , Miss A.Henshaw, Miss F.Brentnall, Miss M.McLening (Headteacher), Mrs M. Hemsley (secretary), Mrs M.Young and Mrs W.M.Smith. Some of these staff transferred to the new Heanor Gate County Secondary School when it opened in September 1964, but Miss McLening stayed to become the head of the enlarged William Howitt Junior School.

Form 1B at the Howitt Secondary School (1962/3). Back row, left to right. Ian Cox, Patrick Doherty, Melvyn Evans, Charles Fletcher, Maurice Lambert, Stephen Doxey, Malcolm Brough, Peter Meakin, Alan Stafford.
Middle row. Walter Childs, Roy Gent, Glyn Oxley, Ronald Gillott, Michael Shelton, Robert Harshorn, David Figg, Mr T.J.Larimore (form teacher).
Front row. Joyce Burton, Christine Hutsby, Jill Gard, Erica Gras, Lynn Harper, Jennifer Hull, Susan Siewko, Marilyn Diamond, Ann Deeks.

The first Aldercar Infant School stood at the junction of Cromford Road and Plumptre Road. It was built by the Butterley Company in 1875, on the site of a farm visited by members of the Pentrich uprising on their march to Nottingham in 1817. This building was demolished in 1975 and the children transferred to a new school on the Godkin Housing Estate at Aldercar. Following demolition, flats for senior citizens were erected on the site.

In this photograph taken at Aldercar Infant School around 1947, Kenneth Clarke, a future government minister, may be seen standing fourth from the left, in the middle row. His family at the time lived on Upper Dunstead Road, Aldercar, but later moved to Nottingham. Kenneth entered politics, and has been MP for Rushcliffe (Nottingham) since 1970 and also Minister for Health (1988/90), Minister for Education (1990/92), Home Secretary (1992/93) and Chancellor of the Exchequer (1993/97) in the Conservative Government.

Langley Mill once had separate schools for boys and girls but these were reorganised in the 1960s into a junior mixed school based in the former Girls' School on Sedgwick Street. In the early 1970s new school premises for the juniors were opened on Bailey Brook Crescent, allowing the infants from Elnor Street School to move to the Sedgwick Street site. In 1985 class teacher, Mrs M.Wright, is seen with her first year pupils at the Bailey Brook Crescent school.

Back row, left to right - Daniel Scott, Lee Bamford, Stuart Spencer, Andrew Booth, Nigel Day, Darren Ottewell, Ben Goodrum, Clayton Clark, Gary Thawley.

Middle row - Debbie Underhay, Brian Harris, Wayne Denman, Claire Guest, Amanda Daykin, Shaun Cade, Melissa Whitaker, Carl Stafford, Stephen Fletcher, Louise Brooks, Anthony Hutsby.

Front row - Michelle Ferris, Julie Posiak, Donna Musgrave, Theresa Fyfe, Anna Lucas, Lyndsey Sisson, Jacqueline Bell, Samantha Hawkes, Samantha Brady, Emma Herring.

Heanor Technical School opened in Heanor Hall, off the Market Place, in 1893, with Mr Ralph Stoddard as headteacher. He held the post for the next thirty five years and is seen seated in the centre of the front row. Pupils at the school travelled from a wide area using the local railways, over eighty per cent were from outside the area, leaving only twenty per cent living in the Heanor Urban District. The catchment area extended from Alfreton and Pinxton in the north to Long Eaton and Sawley in the south.

In 1912 pupils and staff of the Technical School moved into these impressive new premises on Mundy Street. New school buildings were urgently needed as the old seventeenth century Heanor Hall had become overcrowded and the varying sized rooms made class teaching difficult. The Technical School was later renamed Heanor Secondary School, then the Grammar School and is now the Sixth Form Centre of the South East Derbyshire College.

Another view of the 1912 Heanor Technical School buildings showing the many windows and the cupola tower. Groups of pupils may be seen perched on the walls and railings. Many hundreds of local pupils received a high quality education here enabling them to go on to university, college or embark on some other professional career. There is still a strong old students association which meets twice each year at the school.

Pupils in their third year at Heanor Secondary School in 1921. The headteacher, Mr Ralph Stoddard, is seen on the right, with two female members of staff also present. The girls are all similarly dressed and some of the boys are wearing a school tie. School fees in 1926 were £3 6s 8d (£3.33) per term, with Nottinghamshire pupils paying an extra 10s (50p).

The reorganisation of secondary education in the Heanor area in the 1970s resulted in a new role for the town's former Grammar School building. In July 1976 Heanor Grammar School ceased to exist and the premises became part of the South East Derbyshire College. This 1976 photograph shows the final English group at the school.
Back row, left to right – David Lamb, Linda Waterall, Paul Benniston, Carol Mander, Peter Wright, Philip Baker, Linda Allen, Ashley Staton, Deborah Clay, Judith Plumb.
Middle row – Jennifer Thawley, Gillian Alfors, Ian Burgoyne, Elaine Marshall, Mark Weaver, David Bottomley, Katherine Lawley, Stephen Roe, Katherine Bamber, Lesley Dean.
Front row – Jayne Durose, Jayne Piggott, Elaine Bond, Kay Smith, Mrs Pragnle (teacher), Julie Soar, Sandra Stanway, Sandra Martin, Coleen Sims.

Aldercar Secondary Modern School opened in 1955 in premises built by a local company, Vic Hallam of Langley Mill. Prefects for the year 1959/60 are photographed outside the still relatively new building.

Back row, left to right – M.Wharton, M.Hollingsworth, P.Boam, P.Horsley, M.Stedman, M.Thomas, D.Lee, J.Mitchell, T.Boxall.

Middle row – D.Atkins, K.Bundy, J.Hopkinson, M.Nock, S Pickford, S.Housley, P.Fogg, K.Searson, B.Kew, J.Cope, I.Moye.

Front row – A.Dykes, B.Parr, D.Bagguley, P.Lomas, D.Stainsby, M.Abbott, P.Dykes, D.Wain, M.Spencer, A.Marsh.

The Aldercar School football team of 1966. Back row, left to right – R.Gregory (reserve), R. Boot, M.North, B.Slater, P.Scott, R.Judge, J.Ferris. Front row – N.Marriott, N.Hunt, S.Leivers, K.Severn, E Martin (captain), D.Sheen (reserve).

The Aldercar School netball team of 1966. Back row, left to right – Eileen McCormack, Jill McIntosh, Audrey Marsh, Sue Hollingsworth.
Front row – Irene Evans, Edith Wilson.

In 1968 the Aldercar School drama group presented 'The Queen and the Rebels' by Ugo Betti. Production was by Mr.P.Deakin and Mrs K.J.McKenzie, assisted by Miss J.Carr. The story portrayed the people's opposition to a ruthless government. This scene shows a wounded man being brought on set by a guard.

Teaching and clerical staff at Aldercar Secondary School are photographed in 1989. Back row, left to right –
Ms L. Fizak, Mr D. Clark, Mr H.Grime, Mr D.Thorpe, Mr.B.Parker, Mrs H.Redhead, Mrs K.Sycamore, Mr J.Calladine,
Mr J.Handley. Next to back row Mrs J.Wardle, Ms E.Lund, Mrs L.Haslam, Mr M.Needham, Mr M.Horst, Mrs
M.Beasley, Mrs M.Handley, Miss P.Spencer, Mrs V.Gregg. Next to front row – Mrs.C.White, Mrs R.Horne, Mr
T.Penhallurick, Mr.M.Foster, Mr S.Beasley, Mr P.Robinson, Mr A.St.Michael, Miss G.Holmes, Mr D.Winsor, Mrs
S.Jones, Miss M.Farnsworth, Miss P.Collier, Mrs M.Teasdale. Front row – Mrs A.Needham, Mr J.Flynn, Mrs B.Bennett,
Mrs D.Walker, Mr W.Helling (Deputy Head), Mr T.Gibson (Headteacher), Mr P.Wall, Mrs J.Eyre, Mrs M.Davis, Mrs
R.Timms, Mrs S.Ramsden.

44

Heanor Gate County Secondary School opened in September 1964 on a site off Smalley Hill. The staff during its first year are seen here. Back row, left to right – Mr D.E.Jones, Mr P.Rooke, Mr L.Burton, Mr J.L.Hill, Mr G.A.Smith, Mr R.P.Forsyth, Mr O.P.Green, Mr P.R.Crofts, Mr D.C.Lamb.

Middle row – Mr T.J.Larimore, Mr W.A.Cullen, Mr J.A.Ferraby, Mrs J.Whysall, Miss M.Frankland, Mrs P.M.Swift, Mr P.Firth, Mr S.R.Weston, Mr I.D.McIntyre.

Front row – Mr G.A.Swift, Miss A.Grafton, Mrs W.M.Smith, Mrs M.E.Clark, Mrs J.Pickering (Senior Mistress), Mr I.D.Astley (Headteacher), Mr L.E.Warburton (Deputy Head), Mrs M.A.Percival, Miss P.Clifford, Miss J.M.Morley, Mr J.Turner.

Since its opening in 1964 Heanor Gate School (now Heanor Gate Science College) has had only three headteachers. They are seen here at the school's Silver Jubilee celebrations in June 1989. From the left – Mr B.C.Campion (1969 –1987), (died 1998), Mr S.Spencer, (present head), 1987 onwards, and Mr I.D.Astley (1964 – 1969) (died 2002).

Regular out of school visits have always formed part of the pupils' education at Heanor Gate School, both in the UK and abroad. Here a first and second year party is seen in April 1965 on a Youth Hostelling visit to North Yorkshire, under the supervision of Mr and Mrs G.A.Swift and Mr T.J.Larimore (right). The pupils include Linda Musson, Susan Knight, Stefan Komorowski, Roger Beresford, Garry Mosley, Keith Brown, David Gillott, Malcolm Noon, Gary Tudor, Gary Martin, Margaret Needham, John Carlin and Eric Hart.

The boys' gymnastic team which performed at the 1966 Heanor Gate School Summer Fair. Back row, left to right – Roy Hutsby, David Greenwood, Michael Knighton, Stefan Komorowski, Henry Riley, Louis Wakefield, Philip Bosworth.
Front row – John McAuley, Albert Thompson, Paul Bodnar, Richard Galvin, Robert McAuley.

Heanor Gate School's 'A' team were the 1967 Under 13 District Netball Champions. Back row, left to right – Mary Rose, Fiona Arthur, Georgina Leatherland, Barbara Smith. Front row – Helen Cockell, Maria Coxon, Jennifer Hand.

Heanor Gate School has deservedly won great acclaim for its theatrical productions. This is a scene from the 1967 production of 'Ali Baba', one of several written and produced by Mr S.R.Weston. From left to right are Roy Baldwin (guard – half hidden), Andrew Briggs (Hide), Margaret Hunt and Barbara Stone (camel), Susan Gent (Calipha of Baghdad), Christopher Cook (Shekel), Paul Bailey (guard), Mr T.J.Larimore (Caliph of Baghdad), Neil Stanton (herald – half hidden), Mr P.Firth (Abou Hassan) and Glenys Parkin (Sasha).

Another in the line of excellent productions by Heanor Gate School was the musical 'Seven Brides for Seven Brothers', performed in 1989. Six of the brothers, with their brides, are seen here. Back row, left to right – Lee Pollard, Jane Frost, Robert Tatton –Jones, Kerry Eyre, Michael Bailey, Charlotte Dooley, Gary Hoult, Eleanor Hill. Front row – William Bugg, Anna Marshall, Simonne Baker, Ben Brown.

The autumn 1982 production at Heanor Gate School was 'Anything Goes'. Left to right are Robert Tatton-Jones, Eloise Rogers, Caroline Spencer, Jane Owers and James Bardill. Mrs C.A.Baker, MBE, a teacher at Heanor Gate School from 1966 to 2004, produced and directed many of the memorable shows presented at the school, as well as concerts, carol services and other musical events. Over the years, Mrs Baker has also directed productions in a variety of venues for societies and groups in and around the Heanor and Derby areas.

'Me and My Girl' was the November 1998 production at Heanor Gate School. Some of the cast seen here, left to right, are Ian Dolan (Hon. Gerald Bolingbroke), Jennifer Pace (Lady Jacqueline Carstone), Glynn Tissington (Bill Snibson), Carol Lindsay (Maria, Duchess of Dene). Mr J.A.Baker (Sir John Tremayne) and Phillippa Towle (cook).

CHAPTER THREE.
INDUSTRY.

Amongst the many changes that have taken place in Heanor and district over the past one hundred years one of the most dramatic has to be in its industries. Formerly a small number of companies employed many thousands of workers, today a wider range of smaller companies operate but each with a much smaller workforce. For most of the past one hundred years there was work for everyone locally, and even for those from further afield, now the situation is reversed, as many local people have to travel several miles to their place of employment.

Today the traditional industries of coal-mining and textiles have virtually disappeared in the Heanor area. One hundred years ago there were several deep coal mines operating in the area, owned by the Butterley Company, the Barber-Walker Company of Eastwood and the Miller Mundy family of Shipley Hall. As the century progressed and coal reserves became exhausted, the number of working mines declined until by the mid-1960s only Woodside and Coppice at Shipley and Ormonde at Loscoe continued production locally, employing over three thousand people altogether. With the closure of Coppice in 1966 and Ormonde in 1970 the deep mining of coal which dated back many centuries finally came to an end. However, coal is still mined by the opencast method. This began in the area in the early 1940s and has continued intermittently to the present day.

Other major employers locally were the textile companies of I. and R. Morley (knitwear and stockings), Aristoc (silk stockings) and Fletcher's Lace Factory. At their height several hundred people were employed, mostly female, but numbers declined towards the end of the twentieth century in the face of fierce competition from abroad. By the 1990s production had ceased totally at all the local factories and their sites were cleared for new developments.

Old-established companies in Langley Mill such as Pickersgill and Frost (domestic fire grates), G.R. Turner's (engineering) and Lovatt's Pottery were also experiencing difficulties, and, despite in some cases being taken over by larger concerns, all were to close by the 1980s. One large employer to establish itself in Langley Mill during the twentieth century was a company founded by Vic Hallam of Marlpool. From small beginnings making wooden sheds and garages, the firm grew to become a leader in the production of prefabricated buildings, mainly used for schools, libraries and offices. Kitchen units and cabinets for televisions and record players were also produced. However, difficulties arose and in 1995 the company closed leaving a large vacant site, which is currently (2004) undergoing re-development for industrial, business and retail use, under the name access 26. Other local industries, which have now disappeared, include the brick works at Loscoe, gas works in Langley Mill, Harrison's caravan builders in Heanor, and the laundry on Derby Road.

On a more encouraging note large numbers have continued to be employed in the service and retail trades, in the leisure industry and in transport, with a number of large haulage contractors locally and the Trent Barton Bus Company headquarters at Langley Mill.

To compensate for the loss of the traditional industries a number of industrial estates have been established throughout the area offering a wide variety of employment. The two largest are at Codnor Gate and Heanor Gate, with smaller sites at Loscoe and Langley Mill. Businesses range from the making of Christmas puddings to carpeting and from pharmaceuticals to printing. However, none can match the high employment numbers of the earlier large employers, meaning many of the local workforce have to travel outside the area to find work.

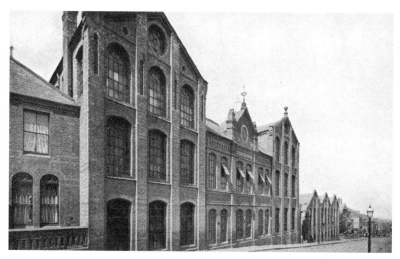

I. and R.Morley expanded from their original base in Nottingham and its suburbs when they began work on a new factory at Heanor in 1874. The company was involved in the hosiery trade but at Heanor also manufactured underwear and knitwear. This is a view of the main frontage on High Street, Heanor, which included much decorative brickwork. The central portion between the two gables was a later addition to the 1874 building, which was set back from the road. Following closure of the factory in the early 1990s the whole site was cleared in 1994.

Further expansion of the Heanor factory took place in 1912 when the Northside premises were built on the opposite side of the road. This view shows the main frontage bearing the slogan 'Always look for the name MORLEY' and the famous Flying Wheel symbol. Following demolition this site was developed for retail use with a number of well-known names being attracted to the area.

Discipline was very strict at the Morley factories, particularly with regard to time keeping and poor work. Late arrival would almost certainly result in a loss of wages. Therefore, there was always a feeling of release at the end of the working day, hence the happy expressions on these workers' faces heading home in 1947. Just to the right of this entrance was a row of high quality houses built for the workforce and known as Fair View, which unfortunately was demolished some years before the factory closed.

Many local girls went straight to Morley's on leaving school. Training was given for the large number of finishing processes carried out at Heanor. Here in the 1930s we see a class being instructed in the stitches required when doing plain mending. Notice the uncomfortable chairs being used by the girls and the school-like style of instruction.

Girls and women are busy at their machines in the Linking and Seaming Department. Working conditions were probably good for the time but it must have been a noisy, spartan environment. The overhead belt drives are prominent down the centre of the room.

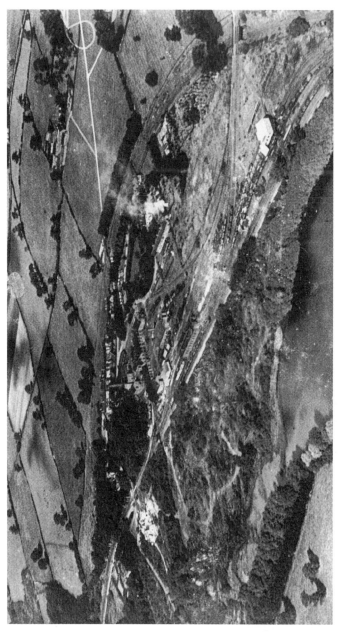

Whilst factories such as Morley's provided employment mainly for females, the coal mines were almost wholly a male preserve. Here we see a 1920s aerial view of some of the Shipley collieries, the first mines here dating from around 1817. The colliery offices, seen in the centre of the photograph, now form part of the Michael House School, where pupils are educated according to the principles of Rudolph Steiner. The school moved to Shipley in 1977 from its former site on Heanor Road, Ilkeston. The area around the lake (lower foreground) now forms part of the American Adventure theme park.

Many villages on the coalfield had their own colliery, which often led to the growth of the settlement. This was true of Loscoe which once possessed two collieries - Old Loscoe and Ormonde, the former being seen in this view. Following closure of Old Loscoe in 1933 the site remained undeveloped until 1962 when it was levelled and made part of the Charles Hill Playing Fields, named after a local farmer and land-owner.

Woodside and Coppice Collieries were the two largest mines at Shipley. Woodside opened in 1847 and Coppice in 1875. Production continued for the next ninety one years until closure came in 1966. Following extensive opencast working around the two mines the former Shipley Estate was opened in 1974 as Shipley Country Park. The Visitor Centre and Ramblers' Restaurant occupy the same site as the former Coppice Colliery.

James Calvert founded a pottery on Station Road at Langley Mill in 1865, making mainly domestic stoneware. The pottery later passed through various ownerships until 1959 when it was acquired by Denby Pottery. The last firing took place in December 1982; following demolition, the site was developed for retail use. Today the items produced at Langley Mill are much sought after by collectors.

During its long existence an extremely wide range of pottery items was produced, from everyday household ware to beautifully decorated vases and bowls. This is a page from a 1914 leaflet showing some of the designs and shapes available for the display of plants and flowers. A twenty-eight inch high pedestal with a seven inch bowl retailed then for £1 9s. (£1.45).

The firm of Vic Hallam began at Marlpool in the 1920s, when the three Hallam brothers began the construction of wooden sheds, garages, etc. A new site at Langley Mill was purchased in 1936 and a large factory built, but, before the Hallam's could move in, it was taken over by Collaro's for war work. In 1946 the brothers finally regained the use of their premises, creating a very successful company, which went on to manufacture a wide range of timber-based products, ranging in size from television cabinets to homes and prefabricated buildings. Closure came in 1995 and the site is now being redeveloped for business and retail use.

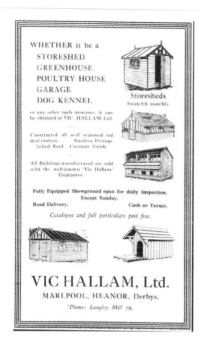

A 1930s advertisement for Vic Hallam Ltd. when still based in Marlpool. At that time the firm concentrated on domestic wooden buildings such as sheds and poultry houses.

The engineering firm of G.R.Turner began on a site at the end of East View Terrace, Langley Mill, before crossing the railway in 1874 to land where there was room for expansion. The company was engaged in the manufacture of railway rolling stock, as well as all forms of steel construction and the casting of items, such as grate covers, lamp standards, etc. for local authorities. Ownership passed to United Steel in 1961, but final closure came in 1980. Heanor Haulage now occupies much of the site.

G.R.Turner's made a variety of railway wagons, both for use in this country and overseas. However, the production of railway wagons had ceased by 1960, one year before the company became part of United Steel. This example shows a twenty ton hopper wagon, used for carrying a variety of minerals. Turner's had a long association with railways, as they produced a large number of narrow gauge vehicles for use in France during the First World War.

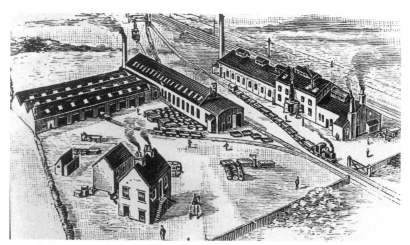

This line drawing shows industrial premises at the end of East View Terrace, Langley Mill, with connections to the adjacent Erewash Valley railway line. The site has had a long history of varied industrial use. It was first occupied by G.R.Turner's and then Pickersgill and Frost, who manufactured fire grates and kitchen ranges. Following closure of this company in 1969, Canlin Castings took over the site and continue to this day.

A.E.Allen established a factory on North Street, Langley Mill, in 1920, for the manufacture of fully fashioned silk stockings, under the brand name, Aristoc. More factory buildings were added along North Street and Thompson Street as the company prospered. This 1950s aerial view shows Aristoc at almost its maximum extent. In 1966 the company became part of the Courtauld Group, but in the 1990s production was moved to Belper. The factory premises were demolished in 2002/3 and new homes have been built on the site.

Members of the Fletcher family began lace making in the early nineteenth century, using small premises in the Tag Hill area of Derby Road, Heanor. In 1838 a three-storey factory was built nearer to Red Lion Square. This was later incorporated into the Morley factory, as Fletcher's had moved their business in 1904 to a larger site at Heanor Gate, close to the Great Northern railway station. This aerial view shows further extensions to the factory in the 1960s, covering the site of the former railway station and goods yard, which by then had closed. The lace factory itself ceased production in the 1990s and now the buildings have other industrial uses.

Heanor and its neighbouring villages have produced many well-known building firms and names such as Oldershaw, Wood and Durow have earned respect for their craftsmanship. Here we see employees of another respected local company, Frank Sisson and Sons Ltd. of Langley Mill. Founded in 1899 the firm went on to erect many well-known local buildings, such as St Luke's Church, Loscoe, the Rex cinema, Eastwood and Aristoc's new factory at Langley Mill, as well as hundreds of council houses in the area.

Heanor Laundry occupied premises on Derby Road, Heanor, originally built as a lace factory in 1875. The change to a laundry was made in 1890 when Thomas Marshall acquired the site. He lived at Parkfields, the large house in the distance on the far right of the photograph. This 1910 scene shows many horse drawn vehicles engaged on deliveries in the local area. Following closure the buildings were put to other uses before being destroyed by fire in 1975. The site has now been developed for new homes.

The firm of Matthew Walker began the manufacture of biscuits and jams in the early 1900s on Exeter Street in Derby. After many successful years the company was forced to look for new premises in 1968 and the decision was taken to move to a new factory on the Heanor Gate Industrial Estate. Today the firm of Matthew Walker is best known for its Christmas puddings, which are sold world-wide and made all through the year to meet the Christmas demand. Elaine Coope (left) and Kelly Smith are seen in 1985 mixing the ingredients for more puddings.

Farming is the oldest industry in the area and there has always been around Heanor a large number of working farms, varying in size from a few acres to many hundreds. Most are in family ownership, often going back for many generations, while others in the past have been estate farms, such as those belonging to the Butterley Company or the Miller Mundy family of Shipley. However, long gone are the days when family and friends helped out at busy times like harvest and hay-making, as is happening on this farm at Langley.

This old farmhouse was at Brook Farm, Loscoe, originally built in 1616, and for long in the ownership of the Holmes family. They have farmed here for over one hundred and thirty years, originally renting the property from the Hunters of Kilburn Hall, before purchasing it in 1919. Members of the Holmes family are seen posing outside the old farmhouse. It was a very spacious building consisting of five bedrooms, four attics, three sitting rooms, a house place, kitchen, three dairies, a pantry and a large cellar. Unfortunately it became badly affected by mining subsidence and was demolished in 1960. It has been replaced by a more modern style farmhouse.

CHAPTER FOUR.
RECREATION.

No-one living one hundred years ago could have foreseen the dramatic changes that were to affect people's social lives and the ways use would be made of leisure time. Then, entertainment was predominantly home-based, with families either reading, enjoying parlour games or playing musical instruments. Cinema and gramophones were still in their infancy, while radio and television were far into the future.

Children enjoyed playing street games or exploring the local countryside. Adults could partake in various sports, as many chapels, public houses and companies had their own football, cricket and hockey teams. The local churches and chapels arranged social and educational events to occupy the long winter evenings, perhaps a lecture with lantern slides or a musical concert. In the summer there would be parades in the town, treats of various kinds and maybe an outing by train to the seaside.

As the twentieth century progressed a new form of entertainment arrived – moving pictures. In 1908 Fred Buxton hired Heanor Town Hall to show silent movies with piano accompaniment. Three years later the Empire Theatre opened in Red Lion Square, Heanor, offering stage shows as well as films. The Ritz Cinema opened at Langley Mill in 1916, followed by yet another cinema in Heanor – the Cosy - opening on the Market Place in 1922.

During the 1920s people could receive entertainment directly into their own homes with the advent of the wireless, although the early crystal sets could prove frustrating to operate. However, as the sets improved, a wider range of programmes became available, allowing sports fans, music lovers and others to follow their interests without leaving home. Wind-up gramophones were also very popular and many families built up a good collection of 78 rpm records, each in its paper or card sleeve, or sometimes in special albums. Artists on record, and the wireless, became celebrities and certain programmes were eagerly anticipated each week, whether it was the comedy of ITMA and Variety Bandbox or the excitement of Dick Barton, Special Agent. Many local homes received their signal via a cable link from Radio Rentals on Godfrey Street. The wireless continued to dominate home entertainment until the 1950s when the price of television receivers came within the range of most families. It was television that dealt a serious blow to the cinema, causing a large fall in audience numbers, leading locally to the closure of the Ritz in 1957, the Cosy in 1961 and the Empire in 1983.

By the 1960s many families owned a motor car and it became more convenient than ever before to visit the seaside and other popular attractions. Travel abroad came within the range of many families with the introduction of package holidays, although a lot of Derbyshire families still spent their annual break at the Miners' Holiday Camp in Skegness.

Today there is an abundance of activities available to occupy anyone's leisure time, something in itself that has increased over the past one hundred years. For those seeking physical activity there are many local sports teams to join and leisure centres to visit, complete with swimming pools and exercise machines. For those who just wish to be out in the fresh air, there are country parks with miles of footpaths to explore. The less energetic can enjoy watching television, videos and DVDs, while computers and the playing of computer games monopolise the free time of many youngsters. This has become a cause for concern as many children today, sadly, do not get enough physical exercise and miss out on the fresh air and activities enjoyed by their counterparts many years ago.

In an area with several heavy industries it was important that after work the workforce had somewhere to quench its thirst. In common with many other places, this need in Heanor was answered by the presence of numerous public houses. They became social centres and many ran their own teams in activities such as darts, dominoes, football and cricket. Following changes in social habits many of these public houses closed down and were either demolished or converted to other uses. One such was the Golden Ball on Furnace Lane, Loscoe. It continued to be used for other purposes long after it ceased to be a public house, but was finally demolished in July 1949.

The Lord Nelson public house stood towards the lower end of Nelson Street, Heanor, until its demolition in the early 1970s. In 1895 the landlord was Samuel Osborne, but at the time of this photograph was Harold Frederick Kitchen. The inn at one time operated a sick and divide club, another important feature of public house life. People paid in small amounts of money on a regular basis and received financial assistance in times of distress.

The Glasshouse Inn on Glasshouse Hill at Codnor was a very old inn made famous in 1817 when a group of insurgents from the nearby village of Pentrich stopped for refreshment on their way to Nottingham. They were hoping to meet up there with others before marching on London, but their venture ended in failure. In more recent times the old premises, seen in this view, were demolished, following the building of a new Glasshouse Inn standing further back from the road. This building is the one which remains today, but it is now Ce Bella, a licenced continental cafe-bar.

At a time when entertainment opportunities in Heanor were few, Fred Buxton of Langley introduced the latest sensation - silent movie films. In 1908 he hired the upstairs room in Heanor Town Hall to show films and had a board fixed to the front of the building proclaiming it to be the 'Picture Palace'. In the centenary year of the cinema (1996) a plaque was unveiled in the Town Hall with the inscription: 'The First Moving Picture Show in Heanor took place at Buxton's Picture Palace in this building 1908'.

Fred Buxton was in the entertainment business all his life and after his time in Heanor he moved with his family to the Isle of Man shortly before the start of the First World War. He set up cinemas and theatres on the island and is seen there with his family in 1915.

Cecil Berle (seen in 1908) was born in Heanor in 1861 but the family later moved to Oldham in Lancashire. Cecil took an interest in the theatre and toured with many companies around Lancashire and the north of England. He never forgot his Heanor roots and would often perform at charity events in the town whenever he returned on a visit. Eventually he returned with his widowed mother to Heanor, and was never known to refuse when asked to perform for charity. In his later years, to show the esteem in which he was held, two concerts were organised to honour him, when Heanor Town Hall was packed to overflowing. He died in 1937, aged seventy six. Berle Avenue in Heanor commemorates his name.

The Empire Theatre, Heanor, opened in 1911 offering both stage shows and films. Following its formation in 1924 the Heanor and District Amateur Operatic Society performed its first Gilbert and Sullivan operetta there. Over the following years an increasingly high standard was set causing the local newspaper to comment that 'Heanor has a reputation for music which extends well beyond the bounds of Derbyshire'. Each show ran for a week with proceeds going to local charities, such as the hospitals at Heanor and Ripley. The photograph shows the police chorus from the 1926 production 'The Pirates of Penzance', with Herbert Buxton as the sergeant.

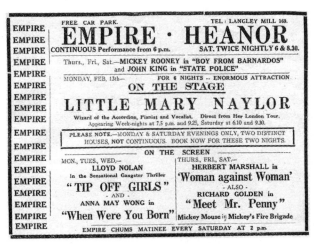

A newspaper advertisement for February 1939 showing the week's programme at the Empire Theatre, Heanor. Stage entertainment as well as films were on offer, with the live attraction being Little Mary Naylor, 'direct from her London tour' performing twice nightly.

During the Empire's life as a theatre several well-known stars of the day appeared, including Gracie Fields and Jack Warner, the latter coming on November 10th 1949, while his film 'Vote for Huggett' was being screened there. This view shows the lower seating and balcony shortly after closure in 1983.

The Cosy Cinema on Heanor Market Place opened in 1922 with seating for seven hundred and eighty people. The first 'talkie' film was shown in 1930, prior to which the cinema orchestra accompanied the films. Due to a decline in audiences the Cosy closed in 1961, but the building remains. The ground floor has been converted to the Cosy indoor market, with snooker rooms and a gym on the upper floors.

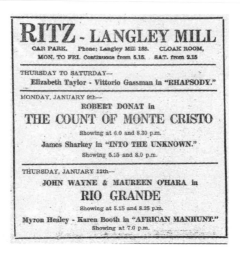

RITZ - LANGLEY MILL
CAR PARK.   Phone: Langley Mill 188.   CLOAK ROOM,
MON. TO FRI. Continuous from 5.15.   SAT. from 2.15

THURSDAY TO SATURDAY—
Elizabeth Taylor - Vittorio Gassman in "RHAPSODY."

MONDAY, JANUARY 9th—
ROBERT DONAT in
THE COUNT OF MONTE CRISTO
Showing at 6.0 and 8.30 p.m.
James Sharkey in "INTO THE UNKNOWN."
Showing 5.15 and 8.0 p.m.

THURSDAY, JANUARY 12th—
JOHN WAYNE & MAUREEN O'HARA in
RIO GRANDE
Showing at 5.15 and 8.25 p.m.
Myron Healey - Karen Booth in "AFRICAN MANHUNT."
Showing at 7.0 p.m.

The Ritz Cinema on Station Road, Langley Mill, opened in 1916 but was extensively rebuilt in the early 1930s. The original single storey building was increased in height and a balcony added, raising the seating capacity to around four hundred. It eventually closed in 1957 and is now the premises of Slater Glass and Windows. The advertisement is for January 1956.

The Carnivals at Heanor began in 1928 to raise funds for the recently opened Memorial Hospital. Originally events were held over a full week but in recent years it has been reduced to just a Saturday afternoon. A parade of decorated floats, marching bands, etc. would wind its way through the streets to the Town Ground, where a full programme of activities filled the afternoon. This photograph is of a float advertising Elliott's Supper Rooms on Ray Street, a popular venue after a night at the local cinemas.

70

Heanor Urban District Council joined in the carnival spirit by suitably decorating some of their vehicles to enter the parade. In 1934 one of their refuse carts is covered with posters exhorting everyone to stay clean and healthy by banishing dirt, using the general slogan 'Help US to keep YOU healthy'.

The Irene Pynegar Dance Troupe performed regularly to great acclaim throughout the area in the 1930s. Irene is seen in the centre with a line of her girls all immaculately dressed. They rehearsed in premises on Breach Road, Marlpool.

Many sports teams were connected to public houses or chapels, while others were run by local companies for the fitness and enjoyment of their employees. Morley's teams went under the name of Gresham and an annual sports contest between all the local Morley factories was held on their own ground at Wilford, Nottingham. Members of the men's hockey team from the Heanor factory pose for an official photograph in 1933.

The female employees of Morley's were equally represented in the field of sport and here we see the ladies' hockey team, again in 1933. As much of the female work consisted of sitting or standing at noisy machines for hours on end, time spent running around in the fresh air must have been something of a marked contrast to the normal daily routine.

Morley's offered many activities to occupy their employee's leisure time, including a Gymnastics Club. Members are seen in the works' canteen in February 1935. George Marchbank is standing first left on the middle row, while others present are Frank Gilman, Cyril Daft, Eric Boxall, Harry Tomlinson, Fred Holroyd, Frank Wilmot, Albert Glazebrook, Reg Hayes and Neville Thornhill.

The Heanor County Secondary School Cricket X1 in 1934. Back row, left to right – H.D.Freeman (sec.), T.H.Millington, C.Colliet, L.Williams, H.Fretwell, ? Nicolson, H.Strong, T.R.Jackson.
Front row R.Maycock, F.L.Allen (headteacher), R.Osborne (captain), L.E.Harlow (games master), H.Madeley.

For a village of its size, Stoneyford produced a very successful cricket team, occasionally being cup winners as seen here, possibly in the 1940s. Players and officers on that occasion were, back row, left to right - Sid Longdon, Frank Worthington, George Frost, PC Murfin, Arthur Frost, George Darrington, Ron Clarke, Billy Longdon, Tom Brookes and Haden Flint. Front row – J.W.Langton, Reg Rose, Sam Darrington (captain), Bernard Clarke and Jack Sleath.

Bowls was enjoyed by many and well-tended greens were to be found in most towns and villages. In 1931 Heanor Excelsior Bowls Club is seen on the Town Ground with an array of impressive trophies. Back row, left to right – E.S.Sharp, ------, Mr Allsopp, H.Crofts, R.Cliffe, W.Bullock, W.Barker, E.Cox, P.C.Daniels, Mr Cleaver, H.Horsley. Front row – A.Boam, Mr Wagstaff, Mr Roderick, T.Naylor, F.Kirk, H.Buckland, B.Bower.

Works' outings were events looked forward to, and enjoyed, by the workforce of many local companies in the days when many did not have their own transport and travel was not as convenient as today. In 1948 the employees of F.Sisson and Sons, Builders, of Langley Mill, went by train to Blackpool, and on arrival they posed in front of the famous tower. The Sisson brothers are seated on the front row. Billy Sisson is fifth from the left, then Frank, Bert and Fred. Just behind Frank and Bert is Mr Everington, chief clerk (with glasses). Frank Sisson died on 26th February 1978, aged seventy five years.

Another company outing, this time by employees of the building firm Wm. Wood (Heanor) Ltd, but the location and date are unknown. On the front row, second left, is L.Searson, third left is J.Bramley while J.Holbrook is standing on the far right of the second row. Heanor Memorial Hospital was built by William Wood in 1925.

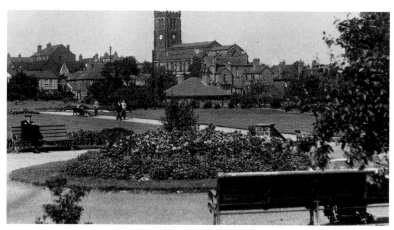

Following the Second World War, Heanor Urban District Council decided to create a Memorial Park to honour the fallen of Heanor and district. The estimated cost of five thousand pounds took a number of years to raise before work could begin. Following completion of the park in 1951, the 11th Duke of Devonshire performed the opening ceremony. Today it forms one of the town's chief assets, a place of beauty and tranquillity.

A War Memorial Park Fund was launched to raise the five thousand pounds needed to create the park on land behind Shanakiel, which had been allotment gardens. One source of funding was to distribute around the town special collection envelopes (one of which is shown here) so that everyone could make a contribution to the cost.

Loscoe Dam has been a popular venue for local people over the years, either to fish, watch the bird-life, picnic or, in winter, go skating. Accounts exist from the nineteenth century of people being baptised in the waters, while in recent years an Easter service has been held there. Many years ago private boats were also seen on the waters of the dam, including this rowing boat, looking rather like a gondola. The elegant hats and dresses being worn by the ladies suggest that an outing on the dam was something of a special occasion, and one needed to dress accordingly.

Generations of local children learned to swim in Langley open-air baths, many having lessons in school-time. Being outdoors the weather always played a large part in how the baths were viewed, being pleasant on sunny days but less so when the weather was cooler. Here we see a class of pupils from Langley Mill Junior School enjoying their time in the water. The baths closed on completion of the indoor swimming baths on Hands Road in 1970.

Like most towns and cities Heanor had regular visits from a number of different circus owners. Here in the late 1950s elephants, possibly belonging to Robert Brothers' circus, parade past Langley Mill church on their way to the circus ground. The circuses often arrived by train and older people talk of seeing the animals pass through the streets or of watching the elephants and camels being washed in the canal at Langley Mill.

A party of Heanor Conservative Ladies pose on the steps of Wedgewood Pottery in Stoke for a photograph to mark their visit, possibly in the late 1950s. Some of those identified include front row, first from left - Mrs Harrison, second from left - Mrs P.Hart. Second row, second from left - Mrs H.Marron, third from right - Mrs F.Barnes. Third row, second from left - Mrs E.Bostock, far right - Mrs Bailey. Back row, second from left - Mrs Latham, far right - Mrs M.Meakin.

The Heanor Literary Society ran successfully for many years, holding regular meetings as well as visits to places of interest. People identified in this undated photograph in the town's Grammar School include front row, third from left - Judy Barnes, second row, fourth from left - Mrs F.Barnes, with Mary Prince to her right. Mr J.Prince is on the far right of the back row.

In addition to all the activities for adults around Heanor there were also several opportunities for youngsters to be members of organised groups; cubs, scouts and guides being particularly popular. In the early 1950s members of Langley Mill and Aldercar scout troop are seen on a camping trip to Castleton. Back row, left to right, John Robinson, Alan Brougham, Barry Richards, -------. Front row, John Brough, Roger Hull, Herbert Richards (Skip), Stan Worrall and Alan Hutchinson.

Recreational activities enjoyed by youngsters, such as guides and scouts, also had a serious and useful side to them, as did being a member of the St John cadets. The Heanor NCB Nursing Cadet Division met each Thursday evening in the former Grammar School building. The photograph was taken in November 1963 and shows Divisional Superintendent Mary Sheppard (centre right) at the side of the Divisional Officer, Beryl Breen, surrounded by a happy group of cadets.

Heanor Town Football Club was founded in 1883 and over the years has won several honours. One of its most successful eras was in the 1960s, winning the Derbyshire Senior Cup in four successive seasons, 1966 – 69. In November 1963 they were drawn away in the first round of the F.A. Cup to Bradford Park Avenue, then in the Fourth Division of the Football League, unfortunately losing 3 –1. This photograph includes six of the team who played that day. Back row, left to right – Gordon Needham, Ian Swift, Derek Chamberlain, Max Ashmore, Billy Newsome, Derek Norris. Front row – Barry Fowler, Brian Fidler, Ken Simcoe, Alan Bamford, Ken Lambert (player-manager).

This photograph is of a 1983 Heanor Town team with the late Brian Clough's son, Nigel, seated front right. Nigel went on to play for his father at Nottingham Forest, before moving to Liverpool and later Manchester City. He took up his current post of player-manager at Burton Albion FC in October 1998. Others in the line-up are, back row, third from left – K.Betts, fourth from left – P.Smalley. Front row, third from left – K.Smith, then K.Jackson, T.Kerry, N.Clough.

The Heanor and District Local History Society was formed in 1968 and still keeps to a programme of eight indoor meetings each year with outdoor visits during the summer months. In May 1982 some members of the committee are seen on a Society visit to Codnor Castle. From left to right are Mr G. Eyre, Mr R.Hull, Mr J.E.Wright, Mrs B.Allsopp, Mr T.J.Larimore, Mr B.R.Key and Mrs W.E. Waterall.

In 1979 there began in Heanor what was to become an annual event for the next ten years, namely the Victorian Market, held on the May Day bank holiday. The aim was to raise funds for the rebuilding of St Lawrence's Parish Church, Heanor. Each Market was opened by a well-known celebrity, the first one being the boxer, Henry Cooper, seen here performing the opening ceremony, alongside Mrs Barbara Allsopp, one of the May Day organising committee.

In May 1984 actor Jon Pertwee in the role of Worzel Gummidge opened the Victorian Market and is seen surrounded by many of his young admirers. A full list of the celebrity openers runs as follows: 1979 Henry Cooper, 1980 Peter Purvis, 1981 Nicholas Parsons, 1982 Jon Pertwee, 1983 John Noakes, 1984 Jon Pertwee (replacing Una Stubbs, who had been taken ill), 1985 Una Stubbs, 1986 Simon Groom, 1987 Leslie Crowther, 1988 Paul Shane, 1989 Frankie Vaughan.

The opening of Shipley Country Park in 1976 gave new opportunities for people, both local and from further afield, to spend their leisure time in attractive surroundings. The Park is centred on the former estate of the Miller Mundy family, who resided at Shipley Hall, demolished in 1942. It covers some six hundred acres and has over eighteen miles of footpaths, which pass through several areas of woodland and open countryside as well as by large stretches of open water, such as Osborne's Pond, seen here.

In the mid-1980s three hundred and fifty acres of Shipley Country Park were given over to the creation of Britannia Park, opened by the boxer, Henry Cooper, in 1986. The aim was to be a showcase for the best of British achievements but the scheme ran into financial difficulties and closed within a few months. To the right of this view may be seen the headstocks of the former Woodside Colliery. These were removed in 2000, but, following a successful campaign for their reinstatement, the wheels were remounted in 2003.

The site and buildings of Britannia Park were taken over shortly after its demise by a new business concern and re-opened as the American Adventure theme park. The new park offers visitors the opportunity to relive life in the old Wild West, as well as experience some of the latest high-thrill rides.

84

CHAPTER FIVE.
TRANSPORT.

One hundred years ago the horse still played a major part in the movement of people and goods. Horse-drawn boats plied the canals while most towns and cities had horse-drawn buses or even trams. In towns like Heanor, many shops and businesses had their own horse-drawn vehicles to take out deliveries, while many professional people owned a horse and conveyance. Heavier loads were moved by steam traction engines and later steam lorries. For those unable to afford their own horses, alternatives were hiring from local stables, going by carrier cart or travelling by train from one of six local railway stations – Heanor Great Northern, Heanor Midland, Marlpool, Crosshill and Codnor, Langley Mill or Eastwood. Some people would go to work by train, perhaps to Nottingham, while many pupils at the Heanor Technical School travelled to Langley Mill station and then walked up the hill to Heanor. Trains were also important for leisure activities and many would travel on the numerous excursions to the sea-side, to London or to a wide variety of other destinations. Some local people undoubtedly owned a bicycle but for most, going to work or just getting around, simply meant walking.

The improved reliability of the internal combustion engine caused a dramatic change in the way people and goods were moved around. Soon the first motor cars were appearing on the roads around Heanor. Dr William Henry Turton was the first local driver, owning a Benz, with the registration number R100. Electric trams replaced the earlier horse-drawn ones in most towns and cities and Heanor itself had an electric tram service in 1913. Very conveniently the route between Ripley and Nottingham linked the villages of Codnor, Loscoe and Langley Mill to Heanor giving local people access to a cheap and frequent means of transport. In the 1920s many local bus operators came into being, running services from Heanor to Ilkeston, Ripley, Derby and Nottingham. There were so many of these small operators that some form of consolidation became necessary. Through amalgamations and takeovers, three major companies emerged – the Notts and Derbys Traction Company, the Midland General Omnibus Company and the Trent Motor Traction Company. The first two companies had their main garage and offices at Langley Mill in the premises of the Notts and Derbys Tramway Company. By 1932 the trams had come to the end of their useful lives and, in the following year, were replaced by trolley buses. The convenience and frequency offered by bus transport led to the cessation of passenger services on two local railways, on the Midland Railway line from Langley Mill to Ripley via Crosshill in 1926 and on the Great Northern line from Heanor to Ilkeston via Marlpool in 1928.

In the haulage business, steam lorries were operated locally, amongst others, by Smith's Flour Millers and Holmes and Sons, Coal Merchants. However, petrol or diesel powered vehicles were growing in number and several local companies offered haulage and removal facilities, a tradition continued today by firms such as Heanor Haulage and Les Wilson.

Following the Second World War the number of private cars increased leading to a fall in the number of passengers using public transport. Again the railways were the first casualties, as the two remaining local stations closed, Eastwood in 1963 and Langley Mill in 1967. However, the latter was to reopen in 1986. Changes also took place amongst the three local bus companies, for in 1972 the Midland General Omnibus Company and the Notts and Derbys Company merged with the Trent Motor Traction Company. The former tram depot and offices are now the headquarters of Trent Barton Buses, winners of the national title 'Bus Operator of the Year' in 1999, 2001 and 2003. The company employs one thousand people, has a fleet of three hundred and seventy buses and an annual turnover of thirty eight million pounds.

Currently, in the early years of the twenty-first century Heanor still retains its good bus links with the surrounding towns and villages while Langley Mill station offers direct rail services to London, Nottingham, Norwich, Sheffield, Manchester and Liverpool. However, most people prefer to have the use of their own vehicles for, despite rising costs and busy roads, they find it a more convenient way to travel, either to work, to the shops or to partake in leisure activities.

In 1779 the Erewash Canal was opened from the River Trent through Long Eaton and Ilkeston to Langley Mill. Later an important junction was formed there with the Cromford Canal (1794) and the Nottingham Canal (1796). The three canals were extremely busy, moving mainly coal from the many local collieries, but declined with the coming of the railways. This 1920s view is of the basin at Langley Mill, with the Great Northern public house in the background.

The Erewash Canal Preservation and Development Association undertook the restoration of the infilled Great Northern Basin at Langley Mill in the early 1970s and in 1973 there was a grand re-opening. Today the basin presents a lively, colourful scene with many boats moored either side of a restored section of the Cromford Canal. This photograph was taken at the Cromford bicentenary celebrations in 1994. Currently there are moves to restore the canal through to Cromford once more.

Langley Mill station is situated on the Erewash Valley line, originally opened in 1847 between Trent Junction and Codnor Park. The line was later extended to Clay Cross on the Derby-Sheffield line, while another extension led to Mansfield. The station saw a mainly local service between Nottingham and Sheffield, lasting until 1967, when it was closed. However, it re-opened in 1986 and is now served by trains running between Liverpool and East Anglia as well as to London.

As an important north-south through route the Erewash Valley line has historically been very busy, with both freight and passenger traffic. As well as the local passenger service between Nottingham and Sheffield, the line also saw many long distance expresses. One eagerly anticipated by young train-spotters in steam days was the Thames/Clyde express, but seen here in the 1960s hauled by a Peak class diesel, unfortunately without its headboard.

For many years the vast majority of freight workings were long coal trains heading south to Toton marshalling yards. Langley Mill also had many sidings for the wagons from Brinsley and Moorgreen collieries, as well as rail connections to a number of lineside industries. Today coal trains are seen very rarely, here a 1960s north-bound freight approaches the iron footbridge close to the former Aristoc factory.

When the branch line from Langley Mill to Ripley was opened in 1895, a bay platform was built for the service alongside the north-bound platform of the Erewash Valley line. The Ripley trains were not well supported and, in an attempt to cut costs, a steam railcar was introduced, but to little avail and the service was withdrawn in 1926.

There were two intermediate stations on the Langley Mill to Ripley line; at Heanor and at Crosshill. Here the Heanor staff pose on the platform in front of the signal box. The bridge carried Fall Road, under which the single track line passed, both to the Heanor goods yard and also on to Ripley The waiting rooms were on the platform but the booking office and station-master's office were at road level, seen above the signal box roof.

The Heanor signal box controlled all local train movements and was situated on the station platform, as also happened at Ripley. Two of the staff pose by the box, the single track route was never very busy, so there would be long periods of inactivity for those employed at the station. Although the line closed to passenger traffic in 1926 it remained open for goods via Langley Mill until 1951.

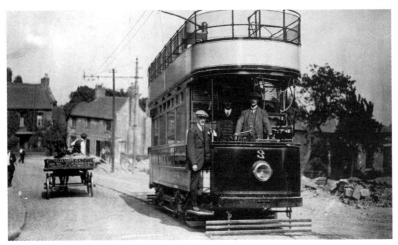

The tram service between Ripley and Nottingham opened in stages, the first trams running in July 1913, between Crosshill and Kimberley. Here we see one of the open-top balcony cars pausing near the top of Church Street, Heanor, on a training run. The trams proved to be very popular with an inexpensive, frequent service and lasted until 1932, after which they were replaced by trolley buses.

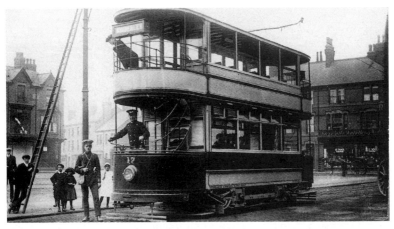

The service was operated by the Notts and Derby Tramway Company with a fleet of twenty four tramcars. The Kimberley destination would suggest that this photograph was taken before the route to Nottingham was fully open. The crew pose for the camera while the long ladder would suggest that some form of maintenance was taking place.

The tram bodies and bogies arrived at Langley Mill depot separately and were assembled in the open. In the foreground of this photograph the tram lines cross the railway line from Ormonde and Bailey Brook collieries. This crossing caused regular hold-ups to road traffic until Ormonde Colliery closed in 1970. The former tram depot has now been incorporated into the main garage of the Trent Barton Bus Company.

Following the ending of the tram service in 1932 the route between Ripley and Nottingham was operated by trolley buses from 1933, with an additional route to Ilkeston from Heanor. The Nottingham service had the route number A1, terminating in King Street, off the Market Square. When the service ended in 1953 most of the fleet were bought by Bradford Corporation, although two were purchased for preservation in museums at Bournemouth and Doncaster. Vehicle number 344, built in 1949, waits opposite the Langley Mill garage before resuming its journey to Nottingham.

The Notts and Derby Company not only shared premises at Langley Mill with the Midland General Omnibus Company but also shared the same routes. Services extended from Chesterfield and Mansfield in the north to Derby and Nottingham in the south. The Midland General Company mainly used vehicles built by the Bristol Company and in 1963 took delivery of six new coaches, one of which is seen at Woodlinkin on a publicity promotion.

The Midland General and Notts and Derby names ceased on 1st January 1972 when the two companies merged with Trent. However, the Notts and Derby name has been revised in recent years on some of the Trent fleet. Trent Barton buses now have their headquarters at Langley Mill in the premises of the former companies. The route between Ripley and Nottingham via Heanor, first operated by trams, then by trolley buses is now worked by blue-liveried Trent buses, on service number 1. Such a vehicle waits near Heanor church before departing for Nottingham.

Heanor's fire engine is seen performing an unusual function when used at the wedding of fireman Joe Shepherd in the 1930s. The happy couple are well supported by Joe's colleagues in this delightful photograph taken near Aldercar vicarage. When Coventry was heavily bombed, soon after the outbreak of the Second World War, this fire engine was sent to provide assistance and never returned to Heanor.

Heanor once had two important coach builders – Hartshorn's and Harrison's, both of whom built a wide range of mainly horse-drawn vehicles. Harrison's on Abbott Street built many residential caravans for fairground people but also made smaller vehicles, such as this handsome four-wheeled conveyance parked near their works. Hartshorn's later moved into the motor vehicle business, building special bodies for trade vehicles, as well as carrying out body repairs.

For centuries horse drawn vehicles were the most common means of moving goods around the country.

With the advent of steam power a small number of traction engines and steam lorries appeared on the roads but it was the petrol engine, and later the diesel engine, which led to a large increase in heavy commercial vehicles. Knowles of Langley Mill ran a large fleet of delivery vehicles, here we see one of their trucks heavily laden with boxes in around 1910, note the open cab and solid tyres.

A Campion motor cycle and sidecar probably in the 1920s. Campion motorcycles were made in Nottingham from 1901 to 1926, but the company was also well known for its bicycles. Motorcycles were obviously much cheaper to buy and maintain than motorcars and therefore very popular among the working classes, who saw them as an inexpensive means of taking trips to the seaside or out into the country.

In addition to the main bus operators, there were also a number of smaller bus owners around Heanor, who ran coaches mainly for social outings. Arthur Cope began running coach excursions in the 1920s. He was succeeded by his son, Frank, who in the 1970s had a fleet of five coaches and various other vehicles for public hire. This photograph shows a Cope's coach taking members of Heanor Literary Society on a visit to Hathersage in the 1950s.

In the 1930s, to relieve unemployment in the area, Heanor Urban District Council employed men on upgrading the former Cromford turnpike road. The quiet country lane was made into a dual carriageway between Langley Mill and Codnor. It became known as the A610 Woodlinkin bypass, as it encouraged traffic to avoid Heanor. Local council officials and others are seen performing the opening ceremony at Codnor.

In 1983 an extension to the Woodlinkin bypass was made which took the road round Langley Mill. This relieved the village of much heavy traffic, especially at the Cromford Road/Station Road junction. As it was designed to connect with the Eastwood bypass, it gave a fast route to the M1 and also Nottingham. Councillor Joe Carty, Chairman of Derbyshire County Council, performed the opening ceremony at Aldercar on the 8th September 1983.

96

CHAPTER SIX.
SHOPPING.

One of the major shopping changes that has taken place since the beginning of the twentieth century is the way in which people are now prepared to travel some distance from their home town or village to make their purchases. Formerly most towns were self-sufficient and people were able to purchase locally all their needs for self and home. Heanor was such a town with a wide variety of small, family owned businesses, such as Lockton's or Holmes' to supply their groceries and provisions, as well as larger stores, including branches of Langley Mill and Aldercar Co-op or Ripley Co-op. Other grocery and provision companies with branches in Heanor included Abbott's, the India and China Tea Company, Hunter's, Burton's and Mason's.

In addition to the main Heanor shopping areas of the Market Place, Market Street and Derby Road, many streets had their own small 'corner' shop, selling an amazing range of grocery and household goods. Other shops were more specialised selling shoes, hats, beer and spirits, decorating items and hardware, for example.

For much of the first half of the twentieth century most shops were open for long hours, twelve hours per day or more were common, while on Saturday nights 10 pm was the usual closing time. Many shopkeepers took great pride in their premises and spent long hours creating elaborate window displays, showing the price and range of goods available inside. A number of larger suppliers delivered foods in bulk to the local businesses, items such as tea, sugar, butter, cheese and biscuits as well as various meats. Very few products came pre-packed, the grocer would weigh out and carefully pack the amount requested by individual customers. Paper was the main material used for packaging, in the form of bags or folded sheets, plastic was still in the future. Deliveries to homes were made by horse and dray, or by errand boys on bicycles, with wicker baskets mounted over the front wheel.

Changes came in over the years, opening hours were reduced and half-day closing introduced. Many of the local family-owned grocery businesses continued despite strong competition from the larger chains. However, it was the coming of the larger supermarkets that finally spelt the end for the family-owned shops. In Heanor, Fine Fare (now Somerfield) opened its larger store in 1974, followed in 1999 by Tesco, who built a much larger store on the former Morley's factory site. The Co-operative store on Heanor Market Place changed to selling just grocery and provisions, but despite this, closed in 2001, leaving the town without a Co-operative presence for the first time in over a century.

It was not only the grocery stores that suffered, for as people became more mobile, they travelled further afield to city centres and the new retail parks in search of a wider choice and lower costs. This applied particularly to items such as clothing, furniture and electrical goods.

Thus one hundred years on, Heanor residents can no longer get all their requirements locally, as did their forebears. Even so, shoppers in the area have never had such a wide choice in food and drink as offered today by the local supermarkets. The large numbers using Tesco and Somerfield show that people welcome this style of shopping and the stores themselves acknowledge this demand by being open on Sundays and some Bank Holidays. Tesco indeed is now open twenty four hours a day throughout the week, something which would have been considered unbelievable by the earlier shopkeepers who were already working extremely long hours.

This 1950 view shows the line of shops along the north side of the Market Place between the Midland Bank (now HSBC) and the parish church. The block nearest to the camera was built in 1902 and is known as Burton Terrace, after George Burton, who lived nearby. From the left the shops were Haynes, the Gas Showrooms and Greaves Furnishers. The Market Hotel has the Hardy's advertisement painted on its wall, while beyond this a trolley bus waits by Rowell's shop, before leaving for Nottingham.

A wide range of small shops with accommodation above occupied the south side of the Market Place, as seen in this 1920s view. The centre one belonged to Bert Hunt, a local photographer, who recorded many scenes around Heanor, showing us today how the town looked around eighty years ago. All of these shops are still occupied but the businesses have changed reflecting today's life-styles.

This tall impressive building stands at the junction of Church Street and Ilkeston Road. Over the years it has had a variety of uses but in recent years was best known as the premises of Machin and Hartwell, Ironmongers; today it has had many extensions and is the Heanor Antique Centre. This view was taken before the road junction was redesigned and traffic lights installed.

A 1960s view showing the range of old buildings on one side of Church Street, a mixture of shops and domestic premises. To the right are Massingham and Clay (Photographers and Travel Agents) alongside Witham's Shoes. The line of buildings further along contains some of the oldest properties in Heanor, one displays a stone suggesting it was built in 1699, but rebuilt in 1800.

Poynters have been butchers on Market Street, Heanor, for several generations. The business was started by Mr George Poynter, seen on the left with one of his assistants. He was joined later by his two brothers, Fred and Ken, which led to other branches being opened in the local area. The business has remained in the family, although today only the Heanor shop remains open.

A slaughterhouse for livestock was situated to the rear of these premises on Ray Street, Heanor. William Hartley stands in a clean white apron in the doorway of his shop in 1909, surrounded by a wide range of poultry. He is being eyed suspiciously by a beast, which has been brought for slaughter by the two men, left and right of the picture.

This view down Market Street, Heanor, in the 1960s shows the wide range of shops available to the people of the area. On the right hand side may be seen the premises of Frost's, Ford's and lower down, Woolworth's. The Red Lion Hotel faces up the street with one of Morley's factory chimneys rising behind it. With less traffic in those days, parking was allowed down one side of the road.

Over the years Boots the Chemists have been located on three different sites in Heanor. Originally they occupied part of Regent House in Red Lion Square, but later moved to Market Street, as seen in this photograph. In the early 1970s they moved to a new purpose built shop closer to the Market Place.

A view of around 1910 looking up Market Street, Heanor, from Red Lion Square. A range of small shops, with living accommodation above, sweeps round on the right towards Derby Road. At the time of this photograph these buildings would only be about twenty years old, as the land on which they are situated once formed part of the grounds to Heanor Hall, which was not sold off until the late 1880s.

For many years Soar Brothers occupied Regent House in Red Lion Square, selling parts for plumbers and heating engineers, as well as paint and hardware items. In this view Regent House has been recently redecorated and, although in different ownership, it continued to sell a similar range of household goods. Today the building has a new use as a tanning parlour.

This 1960s view is of the Ideal Homes furniture store in Red Lion Square, with the offices of Palfreyman and Holland, Chartered Accountants, on the first floor. As well as a range of furniture the windows also display a line in small radios. Today the shop still sells furniture although it is in different ownership.

Lockton's family grocery store was founded in 1870 by Percy Lockton, who was succeeded by his son, Joseph. It stood on the corner of Nelson Street and Nook End Road, Heanor. This view inside the shop, possibly in the 1950s, shows a wide range of goods for sale, with a Christmas pudding nestling among many well-known brand names, such as Nestle's, Heinz, Cadbury's, Rowntree's and Kraft.

Lockton's grocery shop as seen from the outside, with the family's own vehicle waiting to take out more home deliveries. A sign on the wall shows that telephone calls could be made from inside the shop, a useful service as few homes in those days would have a telephone. Percy Lockton was a Baptist Sunday School Superintendent and Heanor councillor, Lockton Avenue was named after him in recognition of the service that he gave to the town.

An open-top Nottingham bound tram ascends High Street towards Red Lion Square, showing the Red Lion Hotel to the left and Boots the Chemists to the right. High Street at that time formed an important shopping area of the town with a number of small shops along both sides of the road, something that has continued to this day.

Following the demolition of the former Morley's textile factory in the 1990s the land was redeveloped for retail use with a Tesco store and filling station opening in June 1999. To ease access a new roundabout was built, as well as a short section of new road to Derby Road. The store is now open for twenty four hours on six days of the week, with limited opening hours on Sundays and Bank Holidays. People are drawn from a wide area as well as from Heanor itself, ease of parking being an important consideration, although home deliveries are made.

Albert Edward Sharman had this clothing and jewellery shop on High Street. He was also a pawnbroker, as may be seen by the hanging sign. Many families used this service when money was short, leaving items in exchange for cash, redeeming them when times were better. The premises have had continued retail use over the years, although the type of goods for sale has often changed. Currently it deals in computers and mobile phones.

At one time even small villages had a good selection of shops. Loscoe had sufficient shops to cater for most local needs, and, in this view of around 1910, many potential customers seem to be about. In addition to the usual permanent buildings, a temporary wooden butcher's shop may be seen on the right in front of the Eclipse public house.

Codnor Post Office on Mill Lane was owned by the Kensit family. As well as its post office business the shop also sold such a wide variety of other goods that it was known as Kensit's Little Wonder Stores. This photograph taken in 1913 shows an interesting Victorian letterbox to the left of the window below an informative notice board. Henry Kensit and his wife pose in the shop doorway with their son to the right.

Cromford Road, Langley Mill, has always formed an important part of the shopping provision in the village. From its formation in 1875 to its closure in the 1970s the premises of the Langley Mill and Aldercar Co-operative Society dominated a large part of Cromford Road. They comprised the two large blocks of buildings seen in the distance. However, the left side of the road also had many small business premises.

Langley Mill Post Office still occupies the same site today as it did when this photograph was taken around 1910. Thomas Cave was a draper and outfitter, occupying the left hand shop, the window signs showing that a sale was on. Note the way all the figures have been arranged for the photographer.

This range of small shops on Station Road at Langley Mill seen around 1910 has had a long history of retail use, most are still shops today. They were typical of many small businesses found around the area, selling a wide variety of items to cater for everyday needs. In the distance may be seen the premises of Piper's, well-known local bakers and confectioners.

Marlpool Post Office once occupied a prime site on the corner of Breach Road and Ilkeston Road. In 1912, in addition to its post office business, it was also a grocery store run by Thomas Godber. The horse and dray wait patiently before loading up in preparation for the their next delivery. The business has now closed and the premises have been converted to domestic use.

CHAPTER SEVEN.
RELIGIOUS LIFE.

A hundred years ago religion played a much larger part in the lives of most people than it does today. Churches and chapels always had large congregations and practically every child attended Sunday School. In addition there were regular activities throughout the week, as well as larger events on special occasions, such as anniversaries or joint gatherings. The high level of attendance was reflected in the extensions and new building which took place over the early years of the twentieth century. These included the building of the Centenary Hall in 1904 alongside the Heanor Wesleyan Church, extensions to Mount Street Methodist Chapel in 1912, the building of Mansfield Road Methodist Chapel in 1904 and the opening of Anglican churches at Marlpool in 1908 and Langley Mill in 1912.

The Reverend Claud Corfield had become the vicar of St Lawrence's Parish Church, Heanor, in 1886, following his father Frederick (1866-79) and older brother, Conyngham (1879-86). He was a tireless worker for the people of Heanor and oversaw the setting up of several church schools as well as new churches in Marlpool, Langley and Langley Mill. In 1906 he was married in London to Mary, the daughter of Lord Inverclyde. On their return to Heanor, children lined the road from Langley Mill station as the happy couple made their way to the vicarage on Hands Road. Later each child was presented with a commemorative medal to mark the occasion. In 1910 Claud Corfield became a canon of Southwell Minster, before leaving Heanor during the following year to become the vicar of Taunton in Somerset.

In addition to the Anglican churches already mentioned, others in the Heanor area were sited at Langley, Aldercar and Crosshill. The latter was built in 1844 to serve the new parish of Codnor and Loscoe, but in 1927 Loscoe became a parish in its own right, and subsequently opened its own church, St Luke's in 1938. There was also a small mission church in the hamlet of Stoneyford.

Despite this strong Anglican presence in the area, one hundred years ago most local people attended a non-conformist place of worship. The Methodists had the largest following with twelve chapels in the area, although they were divided into different Societies – Wesleyan, Primitive and United. The majority of Heanor's Methodists today meet in the former Wesleyan building on Market Street. This became the main Methodist Chapel in Heanor following closure of the former Primitive Methodist Chapel on Park Street in 1968 and the United Methodist Chapel on Mount Street in 1974. Many members of the former Park Street Chapel did not agree with its closure and formed Heanor Free Church, with premises on Midland Road, Heanor. This building formerly belonged to the Church of Christ, whose members had joined the United Reformed Church at Marlpool.

Langley Mill also had a strong Methodist presence with Primitive and United Methodist Chapels on Cromford Road and a Wesleyan Chapel on Station Road. All have now closed and two of the buildings have been demolished. Langley Methodist Chapel stood at the junction of Breach Road and Lacey Fields Road. It was built in 1892, but, over a hundred years later, its congregation had dwindled to such an extent that closure became inevitable. This happened in 1995, followed almost immediately by demolition of the building. Worshippers in the area today are able to attend the Langley Community Church, which meets in the 1800 Christian Meeting House on Breach Road.

The Primitive Methodists opened a chapel in Loscoe in 1861 at the junction of Loscoe Grange and Heanor Road, but nothing is known of its activities or when it closed. Codnor had a strong Methodist tradition too with a Wesleyan Chapel on Heanor Road (1827), a Primitive Methodist Chapel on Wright Street (1880) and a United Methodist Free Chapel on the Market Place (1854). The two latter chapels could each seat seven hundred and fifty people, showing the strong following Methodism enjoyed in the mid to late nineteenth century. However, matters had changed dramatically towards the end of the twentieth century as congregations declined. All three chapels closed and now local Methodists worship in a single building on Mill Lane, opened in 1980.

The Baptists had thriving chapels in Heanor, Langley Mill and Loscoe, and all remain open for worship to the present day. Heanor Baptist Chapel on West Hill (Derby Road) opened in 1876, Langley Mill in 1839 and Loscoe had its 1722 chapel rebuilt in 1848.

The Congregationalists met on Chapel Street, Marlpool, in a building opened in 1822. Towards the end of the twentieth century they were joined by worshippers from other chapels to form the United Reformed Church. The original building had undergone many changes during its one hundred and eighty years' life, but was becoming unsuitable for modern usage. The decision was taken to demolish it and replace it with something that would more appropriately fulfil the needs of the current congregation. Following demolition a new building, for both religious and community use, was erected on the site, opening in time for Christmas 2003.

The Society of Friends (Quakers) had a meeting house at the junction of Hands Road and Church Street, where members of the Howitt family worshipped. William Howitt grew up at The Dene, a large house lower down Church Street, demolished in 1934. In later life William became a prolific Victorian writer, along with his wife, Mary. Both are buried in Rome. The former meeting house is now the Heanor Christian Centre.

The Roman Catholics had a church on Ilkeston Road, Heanor, until it closed in April 2004. The Jehovah's Witnesses have premises at Codnor and Langley Mill and the Christadelphians meet on Derby Road, Heanor. There were other smaller meeting places which have now closed, and some have been demolished, such as the Mission Churches on Burnthouse Road and Loscoe Denby Lane, the Spiritualist Church on Bircumshaw Road, the Salvation Army off Ray Street and the Christian Science Church on Glasshouse Hill, Codnor.

So over one hundred years on there has been a dramatic fall in the numbers attending our local churches and chapels. Many places of worship have closed and either been demolished or adapted for other uses. Long gone are the days when children attending Sunday School at certain churches could be numbered in their hundreds and when 'sitting up' on Anniversary Day was one of the highlights of the year with special poems and solos being performed by the scholars dressed in their finest clothes. Today some of the remaining chapels do not even have enough children to hold Anniversary Services. Also lost are the many activities associated with the churches and chapels, such as sports teams, youth clubs, walking and holiday groups, music and dramatic societies, all of which provided enjoyable experiences in the past for young and old alike. A strong community spirit was often created in addition to the making of many life-long friendships.

This view of St Lawrence Parish Church, Heanor, was taken from Church Square around 1910. It shows the 1868 chancel and side chapels and the rear entrance gate and steps. Some of the buildings to the left of the photograph were demolished in 1913 to allow the road to be widened in preparation for the laying of the tram lines.

In 1978 a thorough examination of St Lawrence's by the church architect, Mr D.R.Variava, revealed that the structure was in urgent need of attention. Death watch beetle, damp and subsidence were all contributing to its decay. An appeal for one hundred thousand pounds was launched to carry out essential work, but later a more radical scheme was proposed. This recommended demolition of much of the 1868 church, replacing it with a lighter, more flexible design, better suited to the church's present day needs. In 1981 most of the old church, apart from the medieval tower and Victorian north wall, was demolished. This view shows what was retained, prior to work beginning on the new structure.

In November 1982 dedication services were held for the new church, attended by the Right Reverend Cyril Bowles, Bishop of Derby. The new structure is seen attached to the fifteenth century tower, which had remained stable and unaffected by the problems that had afflicted the 1868 church. The new building incorporates a church hall, toilet and kitchen as well as the church itself. Its design is sufficiently flexible to make it suitable for a wide range of community events.

The first Heanor vicarage was around the corner from the church on Ilkeston Road, but it was replaced around 1860 by this building on a site off Hands Road, land now occupied by the Leisure Centre and its car parks. The family most associated with the new vicarage were the Corfields. Frederick Corfield came to Heanor as vicar in 1866 and was largely responsible for the rebuilding of the church in 1868. Following his retirement in 1879 he was succeeded in turn by each of his three sons: Conyngham (1879 – 1886), Claud (1886 – 1911) and Ashley (1911 –1917).

Claud Corfield was the third member of the Corfield family to be vicar of Heanor. He is probably the best known, not only for the length of his stay but also for the work that he did whilst in Heanor. During his twenty five years as incumbent he greatly increased the size of the congregation at the parish church as well as establishing other churches in the district, such as at Langley Mill and Marlpool. He also raised money for many day schools, such as Mundy Street and Commonside, the latter renamed Corfield in his honour. In 1910 he was made a canon of Southwell, Heanor then being in its diocese.

Heanor Parish Church Choir in 1912. The Reverend Ashley Corfield is seated front centre, with Mr W.Beresford to his right and Mr E.T.Turner (Choirmaster) to his left. The other adults from left to right are – Mr C.J.Stone (Churchwarden), Mr J.Wright, Mr C.Bryan, Mr S.Walker, Mr A.Beresford, Mr T.Crook (Verger), Mr S.Hart, Mr Shelbourne, Mr Fowkes, Mr Smith, Mr J.Turner, Mr H.J.Windle (Churchwarden).

Members of the Church Sunday School are photographed in 1937 in the playground of the National School on High Street, where JobCentrePlus is located today. The occasion is recorded as a Fancy Dress evening organised by Sister Spenceley. There is certainly a wonderful array of attire on view, with top hats being worn by the young men and a variety of fine hats worn by the ladies, although the one in the middle of the back row seems to be wearing a mortar board.

In 1844 the new parish of Codnor and Loscoe was formed out of the larger parishes of Heanor, Denby and Pentrich. A church dedicated to St James was built at Crosshill, midway between the two villages it served. The Reverend Henry Middleton was the first vicar, remaining at Crosshill for the next forty years. Following his death Middleton Avenue at Crosshill was built on land which he had once owned. When Loscoe separated from Codnor in 1927 St James remained as Codnor's parish church, although somewhat distant from the village it serves. In 2003 both Loscoe and Codnor churches were without a vicar, but the Reverend David Gough has now been appointed with responsibility for the two parishes.

St John's Church, Aldercar, was built in 1871, largely due to the generosity of Mr Arthur FitzHerbert Wright of the Butterley Company, who resided at nearby Aldercar Hall. The church stands at the junction of Cromford Road, Upper Dunstead Road and the road to Stoneyford. In 1922 a memorial to the fallen in the First World War was erected in the churchyard at a cost of £77.10s (£77.50).

A wedding party in 1907 is about to leave St John's Church, Aldercar. The whole scene depicts an evocative Edwardian occasion with the elegant clothes of the wedding guests and the smartly turned out horse and carriage. Unfortunately, the names of the wedding party are not known.

All Saints at Marlpool was built in brick in 1908 to replace an earlier corrugated iron building, which subsequently housed the Sunday School. The Miller Mundy family of Shipley Hall donated generously to the cost of the building. In the foreground may be seen the waters of the marl pool, which gave the nearby community its name. The marl was dug from the ground and then spread on farm land to improve the quality of the soil. When its extraction stopped the hole filled with water, thus creating the pool.

On Christmas Eve 1949 disaster struck All Saints Church, Marlpool, when a fire destroyed the interior of the building. Immediately an appeal was launched with the aim of raising twenty thousand pounds in order to have the church re-opened by the following Christmas. However, the fund-raising and rebuilding took longer than originally hoped. The foundation stone for the new church was laid in November 1950 and the Consecration Service and re-opening took place in March 1952.

The interior of the rebuilt All Saints Church, Marlpool, shows it to be of modern appearance with a large clear east window. Following the rebuilding it was thought that some who had worshipped in the old church might have had mixed feelings about the new one, but their fears seemed to have been allayed. The new building has a feeling of dignity, lightness and spaciousness.

The first Anglican church in Langley Mill opened in 1895 in a corrugated iron building on Elnor Street, largely due to the efforts of the Reverend Claud Corfield, vicar of Heanor. However, the building was soon to prove inadequate and attempts were made to find a new site and raise funds for a larger church. The projected target of eight thousand pounds was reached and the present church on Station Road duly opened on October 8th 1912.

Langley Mill parish church is dedicated to St Andrew and this interior view shows it to contain a mixture of medieval Gothic styles. The choir screen of 1920 commemorates the fallen of the First World War, while the new altar and reredos were dedicated in memory of Canon Claud Corfield, who had died in 1926.

Following the end of the Boer War in South Africa (1899 – 1902), a memorial was erected by the station approach to the four soldiers from Langley Mill, who had died in the conflict. They were Corporal George Tanshill, Private Henry John Lane, Lance Corporal John Thomas Hull and Private William Hull. In 1979 the memorial was relocated outside St Andrew's Church, seen here with the Reverend Ernest Fisher and Mrs Grace Beaver (Churchwarden).

The first mission church at Loscoe was in a building at the junction of Taylor Lane and Heanor Road, consecrated on March 8th 1924. In 1927 the new parish of Loscoe, formerly part of the joint parish of Codnor and Loscoe, was created. The need for a new, larger church was soon realised and moves were made to raise funds and find a suitable site and design. The work was undertaken by Frank Sisson and Sons of Langley Mill. This view shows the church nearing completion, but still without its clock tower.

The church was eventually opened in 1938 and dedicated to St Luke. This is a view of the interior soon after completion. Since that time numerous changes have taken place, including the decorating of the interior to create a more cheerful, welcoming appearance. An upper floor has been added over part of the nave to form additional meeting space, thus allowing the former mission church on Taylor Lane to be sold for light industrial use.

Heanor Wesleyan Church on Market Street, Heanor, was built in 1839. The Centenary Hall designed by Mr A.Marshall of Nottingham was built alongside and opened in May 1904. A Sunday School had been added to the 1839 building but the numbers attending had risen rapidly leading to the need for a larger hall. During the Second World War the hall was used to provide meals at a reasonable price but was demolished in 1972 and replaced by the Fine Fare (now Somerfield) Supermarket.

The original Wesleyan building has undergone many changes over the years, particularly around 1973, following amalgamation with two other Methodist chapels, formerly situated on Mount Street and Park Street in Heanor. It was re-opened in September 1974 following extensive rebuilding.
This view shows the present attractive frontage facing Market Street.

Mount Street Chapel was noted for its excellent singing and had a strong choir, ably conducted by a succession of talented choirmasters. Seen here are scholars and choir at the 1951 anniversary services. In the front inset, left to right, are Mr P.C.Daniels (conductor), Mr G.Elliott (assistant superintendent, 25 years), Mr J.G.Cleaver (senior superintendent, 31 years), Mr L.Harrison (assistant superintendent, 9 years and conductor, 42 years), Mr W.Hollingworth (Sunday School secretary, 37 years) and Mr C.Horsley (assistant superintendent).

The United Methodist Free Church on Mount Street opened for worship in 1858, but was altered on several occasions during its lifetime. A large number of its officers gave many years of devoted service, John Allen for example was superintendent for over sixty years. To show the strength of its following, two hundred and forty scholars and teachers joined with other local churches in a religious demonstration at Heanor in 1901. However, seventy years later attendances had declined so severely at three of the Heanor Methodist churches that amalgamation became inevitable. Mount Street closed in 1974 and was demolished during the following year, the site now forms part of a car park.

The Primitive Methodist Chapel on Park Street, Heanor, opened in 1887, after first meeting in premises on Tag Hill (Derby Road). The church flourished for many years but in 1967 amalgamation was proposed with the Methodists at Mount Street and Market Street chapels. At the time Park Street had around one hundred and eighty children on its Sunday School registers, but in spite of this, and strong opposition from its members, closure came in 1968, followed by demolition in 1970. Some of the members had already broken away from the main Methodist body and in 1967 had formed Heanor Free Church, which continues to worship in premises on Midland Road. In happier times scholars are seen at the 1962 anniversary services.

Mansfield Road Methodist Chapel, Heanor, was originally a corrugated iron structure opened in 1904 and in 2004 is celebrating its centenary year. A desire to build a strong congregation was not as rapid as hoped, there being only thirty one members in 1919. However, those worshipping at the chapel remained faithful and it has continued to the present day. In 1981 an outer brick cladding replaced the original corrugated exterior and in 1985-6 the 1904 forms were replaced by more comfortable chairs.

Codnor once had three large chapels, belonging to the Wesleyans (on Heanor Road), the Bethesda Methodists (on the Market Place) and the Primitive Methodists (on Wright Street), the latter seen in this 1900 photograph. However, by the 1960s attendances were declining and amalgamations took place. Today worship takes place in a single building on Mill Lane, opened in 1980. The Heanor Road and Wright Street buildings were demolished in the late 1960s, while the Market Place premises are now used for retail and storage purposes.

Langley Mill Wesleyan Chapel opened in 1870, but was added to considerably over the years, especially in 1913 when this impressive façade was built. Along Cromford Road were two other Methodist chapels, but all three have now closed. Following demolition of much of the Wesleyan Chapel the façade was left standing for a while, as it was thought that a buyer would be interested in purchasing it. A price of twenty five thousand pounds was set and eventually it was sold and removed.

Heanor Baptist Chapel was opened on Derby Road in 1847, following many years of meetings in the homes of members. The chapel was never in a strong position financially and, even at the centenary celebrations in 1947, it was necessary to launch a fund to raise five hundred pounds to cover current expenses and fund future developments. The quiet nature of Derby Road, Heanor, is clearly evident in this view of around 1910, with the front façade of the chapel dominating this length of road.

In common with most other chapels, Heanor Baptists once had a flourishing Sunday School and each year held its anniversary services. Scholars and teachers are seen seated on the specially erected platform during the 1965 services. Unfortunately, as in other chapels, the number of scholars has declined rapidly in recent years, so that it is no longer possible to hold similar services today, with rows of children proudly wearing their best clothes and reciting a poem or singing a solo. However, the church is still open for Sunday worship and is in regular use during the week by a number of community groups.

The beginnings of a Baptist chapel at Loscoe go back to the late seventeenth century, while a stone incorporated in the present building bears a date of 1722. In 1848 the earlier building was replaced by the present one, then in 1907 Sunday School premises were opened down Furnace Lane, opposite to the chapel. A porch has now been built over the main entrance at the front of the building and the access from the road is to the side, resulting in the loss of the two stone pillars.

Children who attended the local Sunday Schools usually enjoyed at least three treats each year. One was an outing in the summer, another was the annual prize giving and the third was a party at Christmas. Here children from Loscoe Baptist Sunday School enjoy their tea in the 1950s. Parents and chapel members ensure that the children are well provided for and are enjoying themselves. The girl in the lower right corner is Jean Hickling (now Jean Brown).

The Congregational Church at Marlpool was opened in 1822, the stone at the top of the façade was added later and erroneously dated 1801. A piece of additional land was purchased alongside to create a burial ground. A few years ago the decision was taken to demolish the old building, which no longer served the needs of its members, and replace it with a church and community centre. The work went ahead and it was completed in time for the 2003 Christmas services.

The first service in the 1822 chapel at Marlpool took place on the last Sunday in April and this event has been commemorated each year by holding anniversary services. This photograph shows the children and choir on the raised platform at the 1948 services, conducted by the Reverend Banyard.

This photograph shows the scholars and choir of St Mary's, Langley, who took part in the 1962 Sunday School Festival. The afternoon service was taken by the Reverend Selwyn Kronenberg of Loscoe and the morning and evening ones by John Stirland of St Mary's, seen far right. Solos were sung by Peter Davis, Howard and Malcolm Hunt, Peter Crews, Philip Moss, Margaret Stevens, Rosemary Ingram, Andrea Bacon, Susan Smith, Nadine Andrews and Alan Davis. Lessons were read by Ann and Mary Watts, Nadine Andrews, Granville Saxton and Marion Hunt.

The Heanor Roman Catholics first met in 1929 in a wooden building on Lockton Avenue, Heanor. In 1958 they moved to the newly erected Sacred Heart Church on Ilkeston Road, Heanor. It continued to serve the needs of its congregation until closure in April 2004. Seen at the closing service are front row, left to right – Sister Enda, Mrs K.Keane, Canon J.J.Berry, Bishop M.McMahon, Father J.Guest. Second row – Sister Bonny, Mrs E.Hufton, Mrs E. McNally, Mrs M.Hannon, Mr. S.Doona, Mr G.Butler, Mr D.Shelley, Dr P.Holland, Mrs C.Simms, Mr D.Simms, Mrs G.Edwards, Mrs J.Thornhill. Back row – Mrs A.Fisher, Mrs G.Taylor, Mrs M.Duthie, Mrs E.Swift, Mr D.Hannon, Mrs E.Wilcockson, Mrs K.Butler, Miss T.Quinn, Mrs M.Underhill, Miss F.Edwards.

CHAPTER EIGHT.
SPECIAL DAYS.

Over the past one hundred years there have been many national and international events which have touched the lives of local people, some happy, some sad. The two World Wars affected people deeply with the daily hardships and loss of family members killed overseas. Happier times can be recalled through the celebration of four coronations, two royal silver jubilees and one golden jubilee, plus the royal visit to Heanor in 1914.

In Heanor Cemetery many stones stand witness to the young men of Heanor and the surrounding district who went off to fight in Europe during the First and Second World Wars, never to return. Some were members of the leading families in the town, such as Ralph Cyril Stoddard, son of Mr Ralph Stoddard, first headteacher of Heanor Technical School. A commemorative window was placed in the parish church to the two sons killed in France of the Cattle family, Heanor solicitors. However, one local hero who did return was Sergeant William Gregg, who received many awards for gallantry, including the Victoria Cross. A road, the town's indoor swimming baths and a cup, competed for by local school football teams, were all named in his honour.

Something of lasting benefit to the town which grew out of the horrors of World War One was the provision of a memorial hospital, following an appeal for funds. The architect was a Mr Sudbury and it was duly opened in 1926 by Sir Oswald Smith, of the Langley Mill flour mills and President of the Hospital Committee, with Miss Hanbury as the first matron.

During the Second World War several local companies went over to war work, producing munitions and survival equipment for our armed forces. The end of the War was marked by many street parties, although rationing was to continue for a number of years. An appeal was made for funds to provide a fitting memorial to those who had made the supreme sacrifice. A memorial park was laid out on land off Ilkeston Road and opened in 1951 by the 11th Duke of Devonshire.

Alongside the dark days there have been ones of rejoicing. Perhaps the greatest day of celebration locally during the past one hundred years was on June 25th 1914 when Heanor was visited by King George V and Queen Mary. Throughout the day crowds gathered on the Market Place and alongside the route in anticipation of the royal visit.

Some of these special days and events are now recalled through photographs taken at the time.

The coronation of King George V took place on Thursday 22nd June 1911 and here we see three Codnor residents standing outside their decorated home. The premises on High Street belonged to J.Sheldon, who advertised himself as 'Decorator, Paper Hanger and Sign Writer'. On either side of an upstairs window may be seen portraits of King George and Queen Mary. Almost three years to the day after the coronation, the royal couple were to visit the area, pausing in Heanor. (Perhaps the patriotic Mr Sheldon was in the crowd!).

This view was taken during the royal visit to Heanor on Thursday the 25th of June 1914. Mrs Cockle is seen standing outside her decorated Mundy Street home awaiting the arrival of the King. The royal cars travelled from Ilkeston along Ilkeston Road, Mundy Street and Ray Street to the Market Place, where a short stop was made.

The royal party arrived on Heanor Market Place at around 4 pm. Crowds had been gathering for most of the day, many travelling on the new trams. School children were taken out of school for the special occasion, the only time it is definitely recorded that a reigning monarch has visited the town. However, Codnor Castle saw visits from Edward 1 in 1291 and his son, Edward 11, in 1322, while Edward V11 paid a private visit to Shipley Hall in 1904.

The King, wearing a trilby hat, is seen seated in the first car behind the white liveried chauffeur. He did not alight from the car, but is recorded as saying that it gave him 'the greatest possible pleasure to come to Heanor'. Some of the local council members and other dignitaries stepped forward to be presented to the King, including John Holmes, Heanor's 'grand old man'. He was then aged ninety four, being a respected former businessman, councillor and Wesleyan church officer.

Moving away from the Market Place, the royal cavalcade passed more cheering crowds outside the premises of Charles Rowell, later a department store of the Langley Mill and Aldercar Co-operative Society. As the royal car passed on its way to Eastwood and Nottingham, the King repeatedly raised his hat to acknowledge the cheering crowds.

With the outbreak of the First World War in 1914 the Market Place is seen in more sombre mood, only a few months after the royal visit, as a detachment of the local Sherwood Foresters regiment parades before a large crowd. The regiment toured the local area encouraging young men to enlist and go to fight in Europe.

Sergeant William Gregg of Heanor was a miner at Shipley Collieries before enlisting in 1915 in the Rifle Brigade. Serving in France he showed great courage and became the first serviceman to be awarded the three highest medals for gallantry – the Military Medal (March 1917), the Distinguished Conduct Medal (November 1917) and the Victoria Cross (June 1918). He is seen being presented with the latter by King George V in France in 1918.

When the Heanor indoor swimming baths opened in 1970, they were named the William Gregg VC Baths in recognition of the great courage shown by a local man in the First World War. After the War William Gregg returned to his former employment at the Shipley Collieries, only retiring in 1959, when his health began to deteriorate. He died in 1969, aged seventy nine years, but his widow lived to be over one hundred.

A large crowd has assembled on Heanor Market Place facing a raised stage, on which are seated a number of official-looking figures. The absence of the Cosy cinema indicates a date before 1922 and the presence of a temporary cenotaph suggests that it was a fund raising event for a permanent war memorial to those who fell in the 1914–18 War. By 1922 the present war memorial had been erected in front of the parish church.

1935 was a time for rejoicing as the country celebrated the Silver Jubilee of the reign of King George V. The line of shops making up Burton Terrace on the north side of Heanor Market Place is covered in bunting and the lettering identifies the occasion. However, few people are around to admire the decorations and the shops appear to be closed, so perhaps everyone was attending one of the many local events organised to mark the occasion.

HEANOR URBAN DISTRICT COUNCIL (HEANOR WARD).

Coronation Celebrations.

OLD AGE PENSIONERS' & WIDOWS' TEA

TOWN HALL, HEANOR, on THURSDAY, MAY 13th, 1937.

At 3.30 p.m.   Concert at 3.30 p.m. prompt.

Those invited are requested to try and attend.   In case of illness, Tea may be sent for between 2 and 3 p.m.
Please bring your knife, fork, and spoon.   Not Transferable.

GOD BLESS THEIR MAJESTIES.

Only two years after the 1935 Silver Jubilee celebrations the country was again marking a special royal occasion. Following the death of King George V in 1936, and the abdication of his eldest son, Edward V111, his second son, also named George, was crowned king in May 1937. To celebrate the coronation Heanor Urban District Council organised a tea and concert in the Town Hall for pensioners and widows. Here we see one of the special invitations.

The residents of Kingsway, Heanor, celebrated the 1937 Coronation by going on a coach outing, although the destination is unknown. Around eighty children and adults pose before boarding their Midland General coaches.

With the outbreak of the Second World War in September 1939 many local manufacturing companies went over to war work. This view shows work on one floor of the Aristoc building at Langley Mill, where components were being prepared. Aristoc made balloons, dinghies and Mae West life jackets as well as continuing to produce stockings. The Mae West life-saving waistcoat was seen as Aristoc's 'bread and butter' job, over one hundred and five thousand had been made by the end of the war.

Workers at Aristoc, Langley Mill, are seen assembling single-seater 'K' type dinghies, production beginning in 1941. Eventually four other types of dinghy were produced, the 'J' type being the largest, capable of carrying ten men. In all sixty three thousand dinghies were produced. Bomber crews and pilots often visited the Langley Mill factory to thank the workers and say how their lives had been saved through use of the equipment made there.

Another Langley Mill factory which went over to war work was the one belonging to Vic Hallam. A firm named Collaro moved there from South London and began producing ammunition, using a local workforce, mostly female. The work was long and hard, so every effort was made to find enjoyment outside of work at local cinemas and dance halls.

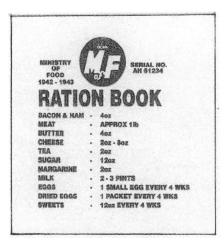

Wartime had brought the rationing of many items, including food. Families were issued with ration books and had to register with shops of their choice. Everyone was encouraged to grow as much food as possible, the slogan being 'Dig for Victory', and even schools had their own allotments. The rations shown here were per person per week, but the amounts you took home often depended on what was available.

Celebrations to mark the end of the Second World War in 1945 took many forms, one of the most popular being a street party, although food was still strictly rationed. The residents of Lower Dunstead Road at Langley Mill are seen enjoying such an occasion, a time to forget the sadness and hardships of the previous six years and share the hope that these youngsters could look forward to a better future.

Another street party to celebrate the end of the War in 1945. This happy scene is on Fletcher Street, Heanor, but it would be repeated on many other streets around the area, as local families turned out to enjoy themselves. The occasion was really one for the children as they sat at tables laid out in the street, being waited on by their parents, although the fare on offer was limited by rationing restrictions.

In remembrance of the fallen in the Second World War, Heanor Urban District Council decided to create a memorial park on land behind Shanakiel, a large property which contained some of their offices. These impressive wrought iron gates were originally made to stand alongside the Derby Lodge approach to Shipley Hall, but were donated by the Shipley Collieries Company to create a fitting entrance to the new park.

Members of the Memorial Park Committee are seen at the launch ceremony for the new park in January 1949. The chairman of the council, Mr T.A.Saxton, has just cut the first sod, allowing William Barron and Sons of Borrowash to begin work during the following week. Two years later the park was ready and the opening ceremony was performed on the 28th of April 1951 by the 11th Duke of Devonshire.

The coronation of Queen Elizabeth 11 took place on the 2nd of June 1953 and, as on similar royal occasions in the past, it was marked by a series of events throughout the Heanor area. Members of the Langley Mill coronation celebrations committee pose for an official photograph. Back row, left to right – Coun. T.W.Smith, Coun. H.E.Parkin, Mr F.Whysall, Mrs H.Whysall, Mr A.Annable, Mrs J.Bailey, Mr E.Carrington, Miss I.Stock, Mr L.Rodgers, Mrs. W.Hull, Mr P.Buckley, Mrs F.Birchall.Third row – Mrs A.J.Warhurst, Mrs J.H.Neal, Mrs W.Shaw, Mrs F.Paulson, Mrs L.Gascoyne, Mrs W.Brown, Mrs T.Carter, Mrs W.Riley, Mrs G.Ashforth, Mr S.Daniels. Second row – Mrs A.Wharton, Mrs H.Hardy, Mrs J.Netley, Mr L.Gascoyne, Coun.J.G.Neal, Mr K.Rodgers, Mr M.Carrington, Mr A.S.Perkin. Front row – Scoutmaster H. Richards, Mr A.Wood, Coun. Lee, Coun. J.W.Netley, Coun. J.H.Neal, Mr S.Hartshorn, Rev. G.Williams-Jones, Mr. R Berresford, Mr E.Harrison.

142

 On June 4th 1984 HRH Princess Margaret paid a visit to Fletcher's lace factory on Derby Road, Heanor. Paul Siddon from Marlpool explains his work to the princess, while the factory owner, Mr G.Fletcher, looks on (top right). The Fletcher family had a long history of lace making in Heanor and, before moving to their later site on Derby Road, had a factory nearer to the town centre, which was incorporated into the premises of I and R Morley.

The Heanor and District Local History Society was formed in 1968 and over the following years acquired many photographs, documents and artefacts relating to the area. It was always the intention to have somewhere to put these on permanent display. This aim was achieved in 1991 when the redundant non-conformist chapel in Heanor Cemetery opened as the Heanor and District Heritage Centre. It is currently located in the chapel to the left of the central tower, the latter unfortunately now without its spire.

The new millenium was not commemorated by any permanent memorial in the Heanor area, although the occasion was marked by the lighting of a beacon on the tower of the parish church. Subsequently the beacon was placed in the garden fronting St Luke's Church, Loscoe.

In May 2003 the restored memorial to the Heanor sculptor, Samuel Watson, was unveiled in Heanor church. It had been removed in the 1981-2 rebuilding of the church and not replaced owing to a lack of funds. Officers of the church and Local History Society worked together to organise the necessary funding so that restoration could take place. As Watson had spent most of his life working at Chatsworth it was fitting that the unveiling should be performed by the 11th Duke. Seen left to right in front of the restored memorial are – Mr R.Hull, Mr B.R.Key, Mrs W.E.Waterall, Coun. H.Longdon (Heanor and Loscoe Town Mayor), the 11th Duke of Devonshire, Mr T.A.Elliott, Mr J.E.Wright.